# Death, Sacrifice, and Tragedy

# Death, Sacrifice, and Tragedy

*By*

MARTIN FOSS

UNIVERSITY OF NEBRASKA PRESS · LINCOLN

Publishers on the Plains

Copyright © 1966 by the University of Nebraska Press

Library of Congress Catalog Card Number: 66–16513

Manufactured in the United States of America

# Contents

# Preface

THERE HAVE BEEN few problems in the history of mankind which have found so utterly and extremely contradicting answers as the problem of death. Perpetually in the focus of attention, death has seemed to some thinkers an unreality, an illusion, to others the most fundamental reality. According to Plato, life excluded death by its very essence, so that an error, a failure in thinking only could be responsible for its acknowledgment, and still Spinoza—in a milder and less fanatic way—refused to think of death as a worthy subject for a philosopher, who should be filled to the brim with enthusiasm for life. But the power of "Lord Death," as Hegel calls him, has fascinated other thinkers, and it is our own time which has hailed the experience of death beyond any other experience, as if life were understandable only when held into the nothingness of death. Kierkegaard follows Hegel in his emphasis on death and is himself followed by the modern romantics, by Rilke, Simmel, and most of all by the existentialist Heidegger, who has coined a formula, repulsive to many: that authentic existence is rounded out by and turned toward death, as if death gave meaning to life.

It is this extraordinary discordance among thinkers which has worried me and which has been responsible for the present essay. No doubt: death in some form is an indispensable feature in life's unfolding; but, on the other hand, can it be denied that as long as we are in form, we do not think of this seemingly fundamental occurrence? Is it only cowardice or thoughtlessness which makes us cover up this important feature of life, or is there a more powerful reason which merges death into life to such a degree that the philosopher is rightly inclined to reject its unmitigated influence? Is the so-called "experience of death" perhaps a misnomer, and must we not instead acknowledge a very different experience, replacing it in the mind of active and creative man?

I touched on the problem of death when still a very young man, and I published my thoughts at that time in the German philosophical magazine *Logos* in two essays (1924, 1925). The problematic nature of the self, its questioning drive, was the topic of the first essay (*Logos*, XII [1924], 393 ff.), and I linked it in the second essay to sacrifice, destiny, death, tragedy, guilt, and a readiness which opens toward world and existence (*Logos*, XIII [1925], 310 ff., 318, 321, 339). Since then forty years have passed, a whole lifetime, in which I have seen existentialism rise, phenomenology increase in influence, and I have, building on my initial insights, set forth from time to time the results of my searching in publications, such as *The Idea of Perfection in the Western World, Symbol and Metaphor in Human Experience*, and *Logic and Existence*. The present essay may be regarded as a small and final contribution to a set of problems broached at the beginning of my career.

MARTIN FOSS

**Death, Sacrifice, and Tragedy**

# CHAPTER I

# The Process of Life
# and Its Immediacy

ONE ͵OF THE oldest questions which mankind has asked is whether, and if so, how, life can understand life. If life is a flow, a stream which carries us along, then it may be that we never get our heads above the waves, but are submerged in the stream.

There is, of course, a certain awareness of being alive, but it scarcely enables us to distinguish between a self, a consciousness, on the one hand, and a content, detached and set over against the self, on the other. The assumption of sensationalists, like Hume, that the self is a fiction, is simply a consequence of the fact that a mere sensuous flux, a mere perceptual process, is unable to detach consciousness from the flux of content. But this denial is an oversimplification and does not do justice to the experience of sequence, of unity in spite of differentiation, yes, of differentiation itself. Bergson has emphasized the perpetual differentiation, inherent in the process of duration, of life's indivisible continuity, its articulation. The paradox of indivisibility and articulation was, however, not fully elucidated, and the twofold aspect of life as *one* process with *many* phases, was even enhanced by the fact that at times the indivisible process in its direction and dynamism, at times the plurality of phases as an articulated structure, moved into the center of attention. And, furthermore, when the content is experienced as a static structure

1

of phases, the dynamic process is dimmed down and absorbed in it, and when, in its turn, the direction of the process is in focus, the content has been overshadowed and has been lost in the process.

We may call the immanent awareness of the unity of process and phases an "intuition" and can regard as characteristic for intuition that it has no *vis-à-vis*, that it is its own awareness only. There is no reflectiveness present in this immediacy of life's experience.

Therefore, life cannot be known or understood in the way in which scientific knowledge knows and clearly and distinctly faces its object, turns toward it, and reflects upon it. Here is only the one immediate experience of flux and structure, in different shades of emphasis. If it were true that the process stood over against its phases as a content and if the structure of phases were allowed to throw a perspective on the process in its dynamic continuity, then the one would reflect on the other as an object of its understanding. But although both process and structure are always present, one or the other is absorbed, dimmed down in darkness, which we call the "unconscious," but an unconsciousness which in fact is only a dimming down of consciousness, enough however to blur the dualism of aspects into one unity, present to itself.

The twofold aspects of process and structure may be exemplified by the phenomenon we call "habit." There is, on the one hand, a dynamic habit, an infallible necessity of intention and processual direction, infallible because it has absorbed the organizing structure of articulation, of means, not open to be pondered and criticized. It is that kind of habit which as ἕξις (attitude) Aristotle regarded as fundamental for ἦθος (character) in our moral behavior.

But there is an entirely different kind of immediate behavior, of habit, which is not the necessity of a dynamic intention and process but that of a stable and static and repeatable structure-pattern, infallible too, but infallible here because it has clouded the dynamism of process and is arrested in a ritual of behavior, of systematized means. This ritual as a habitual pattern also has nothing over and against it. It does not know of its origin nor of its purpose; it simply enacts its own necessity. It gives security to life, not less but in a very different way than the lived intention. It has its main application in the repeated pattern of daily life, while the dynamic habit of intention is the core of ethics and religion.

What allows us to use one and the same term, "habit," in both cases is instinctive and immanent behavior, self-justified because there is no standard over and against this habitual behavior after the complementary aspect of life has been absorbed and dimmed down. There is a naïve certainty in both, although in the latter case, in the static and repetitive ritual, man will speak of the behavior-pattern as a "knowledge," an organized system of technique, while in the former case, that of a dynamic intention of a processual character, habitual awareness will be regarded not as a knowledge but rather as a "faith." At this stage of immanence, faith is the habitual certainty as it appears in primitive ethics and religion. In both cases there is no "why" and no "wherefore," no reflection in the immanence of life's behavior.

It is because of this lack of reflective insight, because of immanence and naïve certainty, that life does not really understand itself. In order to avoid this confession, we may use the time-honored device of identity: we may say with Nietzsche that life is its own understanding, and this answer has indeed been adopted by modern existentialists. Moreover, Nietzsche the philologist has used his professional jargon to declare that life is a text which explicates itself, and Dilthey has called this philological self-explication of the life-text, "behind which one cannot go" (*Gesammelte Schriften*, V, 83), "hermeneutics," a label accepted by existentialists. To be sure, Nietzsche has not always stuck to this kind of identity as a way out. He has at times regarded the "understanding of life by life" as life's suicide, as "life cutting into life," as a kind of inner blasting and destruction, as the wooden horse inside the walls of Troy. But whatever metaphor was used, the understanding of life was inseparably merged into life's immanence.

Those thinkers who have emphasized the self-explicatory character of life have been forced to grant a certain circularity: understanding as it results from life is presupposed and contained in life's experience. The circularity was defended, however, and made into a virtue. Methodological justifications were invented and became the core of the new philosophy of phenomenology. Here the phenomenon of life in its immediacy had to yield results by the use of a specific scrutiny or technique, although in fact scarcely two phenomenologists use exactly the same method. But on one point they all agree: no explanation of the phenomenon is possible, only a description. But what is description? Does it not introduce certain standards of selection and importance? If so, from where do they come? Fear of falling into the trap of alien and arbitrary standards has resulted in the bracketing and reduction of the subject matter, a kind of sterilization. All of this could not prevent a strongly reflective attitude which spoiled the immediacy of the phenomenon and separated process from content, the one as *noesis* and the other as *noema*, whereby the latter was raised to an essence and became the ultimate object of interest to the phenomenologist. Beside this most important essence, reduced and emptied consciousness was doomed to play a rather dubious role, called the "transcendental ego." It is not to be wondered that the most brilliant existentialist, Sartre, influenced by phenomenology, was forced into an empty and purely negative characterization of the ego, of consciousness as a power of negation, a *pour soi* turned upon itself in immanence, and that content, at the mercy of negating consciousness, as *en soi*, was in turn reduced to the ever appropriated nourishment which keeps consciousness flowing in the channel of negation.

As brilliant as Sartre's analysis may be, it is an oversimplification. Negation is always in danger of assuming an altogether much too powerful role. Life is creative. It brings new phases to the fore. It cannot be characterized as a merely destructive process. Certainly life moves on and discards its past for a future which will also have to be discarded. It is ever open, always questioning and doubting, never satisfied in an ultimate answer. Doubt, as Augustine and Descartes saw, is essential in life. Doubt, however, never gives up, but lives a perpetual hope in a future which stretches out infinitely. To regard life, man's existence, as finite and nothing else—as Heidegger does (*Being and Time*, § 65)—is a distortion. Life is both finite and infinite: finite in its destructive, negating aspect, infinite in its perpetual rising out of destruction, its ever renewed process. This may be a paradox, but it has found expression in the greatest metaphysical systems, in Aristotle's potential phases, carried beyond in their actualization; in Spinoza's infinite modes, which are finite as modes but nevertheless infinite in their transcendence and outreach; and, of course, in Hegel's sublime thought.

The paradox of life could be regarded as a scandal by some thinkers, and so there arose a tendency to smooth out the paradox by dropping one of the opposing features. Thus life was understood as finite, as fenced in between birth and death, as rounded out by nothingness, stabilized in possibilities, in projects and life's temporal unfolding as a circular movement of repetition. That in this way life is killed by reflection and turned into an abstract pattern was disregarded. History was equally stabilized by a teleological order in which an anticipated future is carried out in past and present. The props of rationalism were allowed to build the scenario of what was called "existential philosophy": the finite, the circular, the project, purpose, and future dominating time by anticipation —all of the features which Greek abstractionists had worked out and which nineteenth-century rationalists (for instance, the Neo-Kantian Hermann Cohen) had revived long before existentialism was born.

What was neglected was the real passage of time, its processual flow, its infinite outreach, its carrying power, which, in spite of doubt, negation, and, if you want, death, transcends its phases perpetually and gives rise to a belief in immortality. This belief is, of course, only a dim and vague idea; it is not a "knowledge" but instead that kind of habitual certainty which we detected in the immanence of consciousness and which we called a "faith." But as such it outweighs negation, finitude, and the fear of death as a dominant experience.

# CHAPTER II

# The World

IT IS OBVIOUS that the immanence of life—only to be experienced but not understood, only to be described but not explained—is a serious obstacle to full philosophical elucidation. Although life is accompanied by hope and even by faith in immortality, it is a perpetual source of anxiety and of doubt as to its content and phases. Anxiety will move into the center of attention at certain times, which has indeed happened recently, and a parallel to this interpretation of life is even to be found in modern physics, where the indeterminacy principle has raised a storm of concern, while little mention was made of the fact that only the fixed phases and places of scientific objects remain undetermined, whereas the process of their career does not. This process, this career, is—also with regard to life—firmly directed and is lighted up by hope and faith, despite the dubious nature of its phases.

The more man's wisdom deepens, the more will hope, reliance on the infinite continuation of the process, receive recognition. Although a clear answer concerning the meaning of the process cannot be given—for all answers are taken back into the process—there is an objective guiding the process, luring it on and coloring it in a specific way. We call this coloring of the process of consciousness "emotion." Emotion is not a feeling or mood, as anxiety and doubt are, but is directed toward something beyond itself and gives to outreaching consciousness a character. This does not mean that consciousness has changed into a thing—this was Descartes' mistake—but consciousness has indeed received a new unity. What we call a "self" is such a dynamic unity, an outreaching in which character is the very outreaching, and it is the objective for which the self reaches that endows it with a complex and problematic nature. The self is a problematic entity, for the objective is both the self's objective and is at the same time foreign to the self. In its ambivalence, the objective is as much a bridge toward an expansion of the self as it is a temptation and a danger of getting lost and disintegrating in the vast variety of things. It is the realm of infinite possibilities—possibilities to confirm the reality of the self or possibilities to destroy the very life of the self. Possibilities are always turned in opposite directions and have positive as well as negative realizations. For man, the "objective" means the ambivalent sphere of hope and fear.

There is in average man a deeply rooted suspicion against his emotion which may carry him into dangerous and unsavory fields. He wants to keep a firm hold on himself and on that toward which he is directed. He wants to know as an object is known, clearly fixed and outlined and as such *possessed* by this knowledge. The objective of our emotion, however, is only approached at a distance, never really possessed and truly known. The rationalism of early Greek philosophy was therefore concerned only in things, in *res*, and so the reality of being was regarded as a finite structure. Life as a process was lost in this thinglike reality, and so were emotion and motion. Parmenides and his school had to prove the impossibility of process and motion. It was only Aristotle who restored life, process, and motion to their rightful places and proper dignity and thereby discovered the objective of emotion in a distant power, sought by a similar power in man, so that reality was now not a fixed structure but a play of forces: the self reaching out in wonder and perplexity, wooing the power beyond, stimulated by it and sent on its way, but at the same time responded to by this very power, answered and fulfilled, but fulfilled only to be sent again on a questioning drive. Thus the naïve flux of life became aware of itself in the complexity of question and answer, became itself as self a question and an answer, responding by its answer to the demands which the objective put to it. In thinking and willing, the self answered, but was perpetually thrown back into its questioning drive by a power which answered by raising new questions, profoundly problematic itself.

We may now give a tentative label to this objective which is a problem as well as an answer and which throws the self into a similar paradox. We may call it the "world," and as the self's world it gives the self direction and destiny.

The self is not *in* the world, as if the world were a setting for the self. Instead, the self is directed *toward* the world, responding to it and reaching out toward it, receiving at the same time its problematic status from the world. The answers which the self receives will be problematic answers, objective and real, but also colored by the subjectivity of the self and its dependent status, and they will proceed in a continuous interacting dynamism of motion in self and in world, the world-motion shared and kept going by the self's process of a questioning drive.

It is understandable that man, finding himself involved in the ambivalence of the world, in the complexity of receiving and responding, of being exposed to demands which he is asked to fulfill and to possibilities which may lead to his destruction, became intensely frightened. It is the latter aspect of the world as a possibility of danger and disintegration which made him shrink back from the world as a sphere of negation, of absolute nothingness. What this frightened man overlooked, however, was the other aspect of the world's ambivalence, the confirmation besides the negation, the bridge toward expansion and strength besides the danger and temptation. Yes, it may even be that the danger serves as an intensification of the self, if properly faced. Deprived of this aspect, however, the world became in the eyes of bewildered man a sphere of disaster, of utter hostility, of destruction and annihilation, against which man seemed impotent and which was about to crush him. So he reached out in hopeless anxiety, and this became the ground of Heidegger's philosophy of existence, sinister and gloomy, steeped in nothingness and death, while the other character of the world's ambivalence, its power of strength and confirmation, had to retreat into an infinite distance, dimly conceived and longed for in desperation as the trustworthy realm of being over against existence, vaguely divined and raised to the clouds.

Life was now debased and all hope was invested in a realm beyond, in a changeless being so distant and so removed from life that it could be brought down to the pitiful creatures of human existence only by a violent reflection, by a veritable *tour de force*. Not ready and not mature enough to find a solution in a living religion, man escaped into mythology; and always, when man is reduced to frightened debility, he will find his way back into such a mythology as an easily accessible refuge. Even after he has found a true religion he will in times of weakness and anxiety fall back on myth, on a barren, lifeless law of necessity, a fate which releases him from the task of finding salvation in a free and responsible action.

# CHAPTER III

# Mythology

MYTH AS A protective scheme is certainly the product of a higher intelligence than the naïve immediacy of pure living could have provided. The complexity of a self over and against a world is a problem to be coped with. The battle continues between man and a "world beyond" which he cannot possibly master by his own strength. Thus he finds escape in his reflective and inventive power, in the simplest device, in identity as a way out: he forces himself to believe that the turmoil and chaos of his existence are in reality to be understood as manifestations of the never changing iron law of being, which he accepts as fate, and he projects the accidental and disorderly happenings of his life into the mysterious order-pattern which he has raised above his sphere. To facilitate this projection, however, he invents an intermediate realm of demonic powers which in spite of their chaotic irresponsibility are subjected to the fateful order, subservient to fate, yielding to necessity and law, which they must administer whether they wish to do so or not. In this way the demonic creatures are transformed into a mixture of disorder and order, of tricky unreliability and of trust. They become half-gods and half-men, and can thus bridge the gap between the totally reasonable fate and the totally unreasonable human sphere which fills man with self-contempt and mistrust in his own strength. Whether man projects himself and his happenings directly into the order of fate or whether he uses the half-gods or demons as a bridge for this projection, in any case he will be largely relieved, for he must no longer try to work out his own salvation.

There is mystery and even some grandeur in the method by which mythological man loses himself in the sanctified realm of order. He is, of course, only passively received in this realm, irresponsively accepted. But the terror of free decision and responsibility is taken from him, and he would pay any price to escape from his freedom. Perhaps it would not be quite fair to reduce this highly imaginative scheme to a mere craving for security and to nothing else. There is also some devotion present, as well as an urge to find acceptance. But it cannot be denied that mythical man is a weak man who hails the opportunity to be released from the risk of his own free responsibility. Instead of living up to the challenge of an infinite world and measuring his strength by its demands, he resigns in subjection to a mysterious law, appearing in dim twilight and incomprehensible as far as his intellect is concerned, which leaves him in ignorance but gives him the satisfaction of knowing that chaos finds a harmonious solution in the fate beyond. The problem—how life could, in spite of its unpredictable risks, be resolved into and united with a reliable necessity of law—has now been decided: life is abandoned as hopeless in itself; it has to be absorbed by fate, losing its own reality. Shakespeare is very hard on mythical man when he says (*King Lear*, Act I, scene 2): "This is the excellent foppery of the World, that when we are sick in fortune . . . we make guilty of our disaster the sun, the moon and the stars, as if we were villains by necessity—an admirable *evasion of whoremaster Man*." In spite of being an impenetrable darkness, a mysterious naught, fate becomes the foundation upon which the discontinuous and accidental events of life are constructed as they pop up out of naught, coming from nowhere and going nowhere, but held together by the dark frame of fate. It is understandable that especially those occurrences which are at the periphery of life and which are mysterious even for rational man, birth and death, become the main examples of fate, a preferred theme of mythology. *Creatio ex nihilo* and *destructio in nihilum* are the ways of man. The nothing out of which he rises by birth and the nothing into which he vanishes by death are now explained to satisfaction by the iron law of fate. "Nothing" is now the frame of life as well as of world; life and world have equally their birth and their death in nothing.

The credulity of mythical man is a screen which protects him against his fears. His childlike imagination will prefer, not direct projection into fate, but rather a projection into the half-hostile world of demonic gods, somehow akin to himself and thus easily open to identification. They themselves live chaotically, as he lives, but nevertheless reach into the sublime order of fate, which hangs above them and which they only administer but cannot change, themselves being subjected to its power. It is now this in-between sphere which is the most characteristic feature of mature mythology, and the narrative of it—as an explanation of fate—becomes the object of a cherished quasi-knowledge concerning the still more remote sphere of human unreality and chaos. The stretch of this quasi-real narration is *illud tempus*, as Eliade calls it in *The Myth of the Eternal Return* (pp. 20 ff.). In its fulfillment of time, *illud tempus* exhausts temporal reality and is the only significant process with regard to the events of human existence, which only *seem* to be real. The latter feed into *illud tempus* and are to be projected into the all-comprehensive stretch as their true meaning and reality. As such, we are a mere illusion and receive a kind of reality only by being sucked into *illud tempus* and its mythical events, into the narrative which as a whole fulfills time and gives meaning to our chaotic and accidental existence. Eliade is therefore not quite correct when he speaks of human events as repeating what happened in *illud tempus* and when he regards mythological time as the model which is imitated by our lives. Repetition and imitation would ask for at least a minimum of decision on the part of man. But this would be more than mythology bargains for; it is instead true that man, without any action or free decision on his part, is drawn into the mythological setting and its unfolding. He is absorbed by *illud tempus*. His own time, with its turbulent sequence of events, becomes a nothing, an illusion, and loses its reality in favor of the one and only reality which fate provides, a reality explicated by the mythical narration. Nothing ever really takes place down here on earth except a dream. Reality is only the timeless, ever present myth which sucks into itself all the events of illusionary time and makes them a part of its own iron necessity. Man is a mere exemplification of the mythical story, and he cannot escape absorption into a frozen pattern even if he wishes to do so. But he does not wish it, for his being absorbed into the myth-pattern is exactly what pleases him and rids him of responsibility. Calvin's predestination has all the earmarks of the mythological alibi, and this is the reason why even the damned accept their doom as an explication of inscrutable fate.

Rightly understood, there is no past and no future in the mythological view, but only a timeless setting. What seems a past—for instance the curse grounded in happenings of the past—is instead a timeless cloud hanging over man, and the future—the carrying out of the curse—is part of the same timeless setting. And since there is no past and no future, there is also not really any *re*birth or *re*petition or *re*turn, only the revelation that man has never left the *illud tempus* and that what we call "time" is an illusion, just as we ourselves are an illusion, a projection of the timeless creatures which act in the myth.

The ambivalence of mythology has often been asserted, but it is an ambivalence of a very specific kind, not to be confused with the ambivalence of immediate naïve life, nor with the ambivalence of self and world. While on the level of immanent life, the process and its content were intertwined, so that consciousness lightened up first the one and then the other, sending its counterpart into the darkness of the unconscious, and while in confrontation with world, the problematic self was directed toward answering and responding to the call of the world, although it remained a problem in its own right; mythological ambivalence smooths down all perplexities by the device of identity. What seemed chance is identical with and thus an instance of necessity; man's downfall is identical with and thus in reality the triumph of ruling fate; all the shifting chaotic events are in reality the explication of an unchanging iron necessity of law. Thus everything is just as meaningless as it is full of meaning, and man, exposed to this ambivalence, feels neither joy nor despair, but rather resignation, being a helpless and irresponsible puppet. But resignation is perhaps still too strong; we should instead speak of acceptance without any emotional concern. Man has abandoned his self to an irresponsible setting of determinism. He is left to a detached noncommitment, to pure "facticity." That man is "thrown into the world," Heidegger's famous dictum (*Being and Time*, § 29), is mythology rather than philosophy.

The place of myth in the development of man is usually found at the beginning as a first imaginative attempt at creativity. It may appear early on the stage of civilization, at the very moment when the genius of man embarks upon philosophical vision and the dangerous discovery of free responsibility. It turns man away from this nascent philosophy and lands him in the dead end of a playful, irresponsible arrest in fatalism. From here man will have to rise out of myth to a mature intellectual and emotional level. He may find it in poetry or philosophy or religion. But even then, man, weak as he is, may fall back on myth in order to mitigate the strain of responsible decision inherent in the higher achievements of culture. Even philosophers may fall back on myths, as Parmenides, Empedocles, and even Plato did, although here mythology has lost some of its seriousness. Aristotle discarded myth, although he called the philosopher a "lover of myth," a lover, however, who destroyed what he loved when embarking upon his true vocation.

Tragedy too was grounded in myth but surpassed myth, as we shall see later on, and religion, in a similar way, started mythologically and remained rooted in myth as long as man had not yet found the strength of responsible faith. Myth has blocked the road to a mature religion in certain cultures which never reached the stage of a free communion between God and man; but it has also become an escape and an alibi for weak man, allowing him to desert his religion and to fall back on irresponsible mythology. We find such relapses in our own religion; therefore, the demythologization of modern theology is a serious matter and a necessity if religion is to be purified and purged of escape devices with regard to responsibility and freedom. The serpent in Paradise is a mythological alibi, and so is the passive abandonment of Christ to his murderers as a condition for the salvation of mankind whereby the fruits of the Cross are simply reaped without any effort on the part of those who reap them. Moreover, the coming of the Kingdom, when regarded as a mere gift, is an irresponsible escape and alibi for man, too weak to cope with his troubles. All of this is foreign to the true spirit of mature religion as the revelation of man's free status before God, called by Him into decision and action (see Deuteronomy 5:2-3 and 30:19).

There is a certain dehumanization in myth. Man, who has lost his essential character of free responsibility, looks for guidance in symptoms of a subhuman nature, either in life-less happenings of a chance-character or in the equally accidental behavior of animals; in the intestines of sacrificial victims or in the flight of birds. The elevated lives of the demonic Gods too are steeped in subhuman violence and change into animal forms. Zeus may appear as a snake or a bull; Poseidon as a horse; the Erinyes as bloodhounds. Human form is lost with human dignity, and the now transformed demons act in an ambivalent manner, unreliable and chaotic.

Thus the *illud tempus* of myth, in spite of its original sublimity, may turn out to be a medium of disaster, a level of terror. Eliade, who regards history as the medium of terror and glorifies myth, is very much mistaken. Mature religion, biblical religion, is grounded in history. Later on we shall have to broach the problem of history, profoundly presented in the Bible and philosophically expounded by Hegel. Modern thinkers, especially Heidegger and his followers, have deserted the road of history and have, under the very label of history, taken refuge in mythological fate. Here man—not unlike the Calvinist—is free only to become aware of his captivity in the timeless circle of fate, for which petrification and arrest in death become the ultimate seal.

Mythology has once and for all stabilized and terminated time in the setting of *illud tempus*. History, however, lives the ever new birth of events, infinitely reaching forward into a future which is never closed. It is the closure of time which is so characteristic of mythology. Sometimes this closure was hailed, but at other times closure made it difficult for man,

left outside, to project himself into its orbit. Thus when the
passive absorption into myth and its *illud tempus* was not
feasible, man was compelled to make an active attempt to
mold myth, or certain parts of it, according to the human
situation, repeating and imitating mythological events in a
handy, practical manner. Here indeed imitation and repetition were used as a technique built on mythical knowledge,
and this is what we call "magic" or "ritual," a symbolic
crystallization and reduction, now to be imposed on the
accidental doings of men, giving them a pseudo-necessity,
but in reality being arbitrary and moving toward ever
changing and ever more complex symbolic structures until at
last man is drowned in a nebulous mass possessing a tight
texture. This happened in early Christian times when gnosis
enveloped religious thinking in its complex symbolic forma-
tions. The symbolic reduction of magic serves, as myth does,
for the sake of security and provides a handy technique of
irresponsible protection. The fateful narrative of the myth
is cut up into magic formulas which are used repeatedly.
Thus Tibetan Mahayana Buddhism employed various stages
and various phases of Buddha's life in *illud tempus* as a
ritualistic repetition in order to obtain magical results and to
hasten man's absorption into nirvana. The sacramental
rituals of our church also repeat certain mythological events,
such as communion or baptism, in order to facilitate the
believer's absorption into the mythically interpreted life of
Christ. Here magic is a danger to true religion, just as its
source, myth, was such a danger. Not only did demythologization become necessary, but so too did deritualization,
as far as rituals had developed into magic. The prophetic
revolution was turned against magic ritual, and so was the
revolution called "Protestantism."

There is a kinship between myth and a certain brand of

mysticism which absorbs the temporal happenings of life into an *illud tempus*, a divine, unchanging ground. The mystic here abandons himself to this ground, is absorbed by it, and receives divine mystical knowledge. The *illud tempus*, however, is deprived of happenings and is therefore an empty eternity, while the happenings which are important for the mystic become a preparatory stage which leads to the mystical union and is extinguished when union is achieved. The Buddhist arhat, after having reached nirvana, regards this preparatory stage, including the teaching of Buddha, as nonreal, as if it had never been. In this regard, Western mysticism is different, and can scarcely be compared to the mythical view. The earthly happenings are here far from losing reality; on the contrary, they receive from beyond a heightened reality, are justified and sanctified, because they are imbued with a higher meaning. When St. Paul "puts on Christ" or when he cries out that it is not he who lives but Christ who lives in him, his earthly life has not vanished but is now transformed, sanctified in its earthly form. And when Meister Eckhart has the vision of Christ being born, crucified, and resurrected in *him*, it is his earthly life which has become intensified by the breaking in of the higher sphere. Thus this kind of mysticism does not provide an alibi for man, who wants to hide in an irresponsible mystery, but, on the contrary, confronts man with an intensified responsibility because he now feels the call deeply rooted in his sanctified, sacramental existence.

Before closing this chapter, we may mention a weaker form of myth which today is cherished only by children but which has all the symptoms of the irresponsible absorption into *illud tempus*. I mean the fairy tale. "Once upon a time . . . ."—this beginning removes the listener from his historical position and thrusts him into a mysterious setting of its own.

The child enjoys the removal, especially since the tale will show the hero as an innocent instrument of powers beyond his influence. These powers will, however, mix here more naïvely with the human hero; fairies and dwarfs will enter his life to help, while giants and monsters will endanger it, but only in order to be defeated, so that the happy ending gives security to the troubled, childish mind. Therefore, the child will want to hear the fairy tale over and over again, as a repeated ritual which in its exact repetition has a quasi-magical effect upon it. Still, in our time, primitive, childlike people at the border of the desert listen to the storyteller when nightfall comes and fear grips their troubled minds.

In troubled times, adults, like children, seek appeasement and security. Myth, magic, and ritual invade the life of men weakened by disaster and fear. Mature man has no need for these remedies. He uses his gift of reason and imagination for a more adequate coping with danger. He may embark upon the sober road of science, and when even science proves inadequate, he will reach the height of his cultural development in ethics, art, and religion.

# CHAPTER IV

# The Scientific System and Its Failure: The Absurd

THE MYTH SATISFIES child and adolescent. It is the playful escape from the responsible confrontation of self with world. Adult man is in need of a more than playful defense. He may adopt the dualism of an unchanging lawful necessity and a manifold of fleeting, shifting events, but he will try to find a clearer, less ambivalent relation than blurring identity had been between fate and facts in the mythological sphere.

What, however, will this new relation between law and facts be? Can there be any satisfactory relation or will this relation remain a mystery? In the beginning of this new adventure of man, Plato's thought still followed very much the mythological pattern. Not only did he use myths in his writings, but he even gave to his realm of ultimate reality a fatelike character before which the facts of daily life dwindled away in illusion and irreality. A lifetime of strenuous work was required before Plato, at the end of his life, imbued the realm of fleeting facts with reality too. But how are these two realities of law and of fact united and reconciled with each other? Plato had no clear answer, and neither has our modern science. It is simply decreed that the facts verify the law and that the law confirms the facts as its instances. This is brought about by recognizing a law-structure that is inherent in every fact, so that the fact, besides being itself, is also transparent with regard to the law which it verifies. The fact stands for the law, is a symbol of the law, and this together with other facts, all of them symbolically directed to the one all-comprising law of systematization.

In order to achieve this ingenious master stroke, a violent transformation and reduction had to take place: as symbols of the abstract law, facts are themselves abstract and have reality in their abstractness. The concrete has vanished. It is not unreal, not an illusion, but it is scientifically unimportant, for it is unique, and only that which is repeatable counts, because it is a symbol of the general law. Facts which are reduced to repeatable symbols in this way are united by relations because they are essentially placed in a system as the all-embracing structure of relationships.

Time and space have now grown in importance as abstract order-structures for facts, relating facts, measurable in their distance. Movement has lost its dynamism and is similarly transformed into a relational pattern of fixed phases, of which one is cause, that is, a necessity of condition with regard to the neighboring phase as its effect. Systematic relation and fixation in the system is all that is.

It is again the motive of security which has given rise to this new and sober and clear picture of reality. Everything has its place in the system and symbolizes the totality of the system, from which it receives its necessity. There is nothing playful or arbitrary in this scheme, and the most devoted work goes into the detailed erection of it. Once the system is set up, however, no conscientious decision is afforded, no responsibility is taken; the system works, like the mythical fate had worked, without any free interference by man. There is only total determination.

What is accomplished in this manner is the mastering of a lifeless environment for practical use. Life, with which man started and which had been his main concern, has been squeezed out of the system. Self, world, communion, and dynamic process have disappeared. Plato was uncertain about what status he should give to the soul and to Eros; they were neither laws nor facts. Even in our time the scientific system falls short when life, self, and world are at stake.

In this situation man feels uneasy in spite of the limited security which the system provides. He has omitted life from his system, and so life, left out, seems to be threatened. Science tries hard to forget its insular and reduced character of abstract fixation and to usurp the full responsibility for truth. But this attempt breaks down when life knocks at the wall of the system, and the scientist, in an era of atomic energy, cannot possibly deny that he has undermined life, that his findings may at any time blast life sky high. He is forced to ask himself whether the ultimate standard of truth, even scientific truth, should not be that very life which he has forgotten, and whether a science which instead of serving life endangers it is not a deficient science, an untruth when seen in the perspective of life. But here we are faced with an unexpected phenomenon: the prophets of life, the poets, painters, musicians, and philosophers of today do not defend life against the threatening system of reduction and petrification. They too look at life as does the scientist and regard it as being outside the system and therefore *absurd*. The absurdity of life is not felt with dismay, as one would expect, but is accepted as inevitable, yes, it has become a title of honor, is regarded by artists and poets as a value in its own right. Life fascinates because it is absurd. It is certainly a failure, for it cannot be fully elucidated by reason: it is inevitable that our longing for rational clarity clashes with the "wall of the world," as Camus puts it. Life as absurd is a *rencontre* with reason, as Sartre declares, and it loses in this *rencontre*; it is *de trop*, something which does not balance in the total account of reality (*La Nausée*, pp. 160 ff.). In *Le Mythe de Sisyphe*, Camus attempts to analyze the absurd by linking it to the terrifying event of death. Death appears as the seal on the absurdity of life. What Camus means here, however, is not death as an experience and reality, for he concedes that death as such can never be experienced (*Le Mythe de Sisyphe*, p. 30); it is the accidental breaking in of death into life, the chance-element, which renders life absurd. This absurd chance must be accepted, according to Camus, although it is the "supreme abuse"; no escape from the absurd into faith is permitted, nor is escape into suicide, and the latter prohibition makes it fully clear that it is not death as such which is the stamp of absurdity. Absurd is any accidental happening, any chance-event which, somehow defying the continuity of life, is experienced in this its obstructive character by life's own perspective. Death as such cannot be experienced; it is an unknowable factor outside life, an enigma, nothing more. The absurd passes death by, and so does reason. But chance enters life as a hostile and inhuman factor and delivers man into the trap of the absurd (see also Sartre, *Being and Nothingness*, p. 533).

We would expect man to turn away from absurdity and chance in disgust. Why, then, does Camus ask us to accept them and even to revolt against any escape from the absurd? Camus believes that only acceptance makes us masters of our destiny. Sisyphus, Camus tells us, is happy because he has accepted his absurd destiny, the ever repeated accident of the slipping rock, slipping out of his hands so that he must roll it up the hill again and again. This is the "dark horizon," which engulfs man in a protective cloud, freeing him from hope and tomorrow. We shall live a discontinuous life from moment to moment, unattached, indifferent, receiving thus a kind of reconciliation or, better, a kind of unpierceable armor against the absurd, a mysterious realm which Sartre calls in *La Nausée* the *secret de l'existence*, a secret which, however, as secret, is discussed and communicated in books and lectures.

As much as Camus and Sartre bring the absurd near to mythology, there is a definite difference here. While in mythology the necessity of fate is of utter importance and prevails over the realm of chance, it is the absurd which reverses the emphasis. In absurdity the chance rules, the unpredictable breaks the fetters of law, and although, as in the mythological realm, a certain identity is upheld between necessity and chance, it is chance which in this identity gives its mark to the whole realm.

When, therefore, death appears as a manifestation of the absurd, it is not the biological necessity of death which is at stake. It is rather the accidental ingression of death into life, its unpredictable advent in the course of events. In this way death "dissolves nemesis," as Camus tells us, and is a reconciliation, even a happiness. It is indeed a relief for man that he cannot predict the hour of death and that young and old alike are equally exposed to a death which may come at any time. That an absurd chance-event cannot fill man's heart with a serious concern is obvious.

If the absurd in Sartre's and Camus' writings was brought near to myth, the absurd in Kafka's work is connected with ritual and magic rather than with mythology. The absurd ritual, inefficient and inept to take care of the believer, fools and traps and finally destroys him. In *The Trial*, as well as in *The Castle*, man is confronted by a distant and incomprehensible structure, a sophistic, symbolic pattern, a ritual and magic, to which he submits and which in all its absurdity conveys dignity to him. He even feels contempt for those who are outside the ritual. Here is no revolt or defiance, but a confused submission to the ritual, a naïve, childlike credulity, in spite of the ritual's evasive and inefficient nature. In two legends Kafka gives us an insight into this inefficiency. In one of them a man waits all his life before the door to heaven, but—although this is the door reserved for *his* and only *his* salvation—the door remains unapproachable and is finally closed after he has died. The other legend tells us about a ruler who lives in a palace so vast that neither can he get his messages out to his subjects nor can the subjects get to him. Absurdity is found also in death, which here, as with Camus, has an element of justification with regard to life. The unfinished novel *The Castle* was intended to end with a justification of life's absurdity by death, a death, however, which was not at the end of life as a necessary biological event but which was present throughout the process of life as an absurd meaning inherent in life as such. The right to live can only be revealed by death (Wilhelm Emrich, *Franz Kafka*, p. 410).

It is of no small importance that we come upon death in our essay not only as a mythological theme but also as an event of supreme absurdity, and this absurdity is manifested in chance as well as in a confusing ritual. What we may call the "experience of death" is therefore rather the experience of chance and confusion throughout life. A direct experience of death as such has not yet been met, and so we may withhold assent to such an experience until we have dug deeper into its claim.

The absurd is not restricted to literature. It also invades the realm of modern fine arts and music. But it is not openly acknowledged and does not undergo a marriage with myth or magic. It is instead true that life surrenders in art and music to the intellectual system as such, reducing art's scope so that it fits into the rational pattern of abstraction. Here the absurd

is that life is violently hostile toward itself, eliminates itself
for the sake of abstract geometrical structures. What is
called "nonrepresentative art" is not really without subject
matter. Art must always represent something. But what this
form of art refuses to represent is life in its dynamic and
continuous unfolding: mood in nature, life in human bodies
and faces. In its bewildered state, art now tries to fulfill what
science has begun—to exclude life and to regard it as unfit
for representation. We see the young Picasso in his *Demoi-
selles d'Avignon* violently destroy the living forms and change
them into angular geometrical patterns, as if the young
ladies had been beaten into this distortion. In his famous
mural *Guernica*, the debris of human bodies—in fact of
plaster statues caricaturing life—is strewn over the canvas,
allowing only abstract design to articulate the surface of the
picture. The hostility toward life is unparalleled. Picasso
declares that "pictures are weapons against the enemy."
The real enemy for such artists is life, unpredictable by reason
and confusing in its abundance. The subject matter which
now substitutes for the richness of life is intentionally poor
and allows only a routine of ever repeated patterns. That the
geometry in some of these works has retained a remnant of
dynamism, that the angry furor of destruction still has a
simmering of life, a minimum of rhythm, this and only this
saves them from total oblivion. Life, petrified and enslaved,
still revolts in these works and accuses their originator of his
sin against life. It is this trembling of life beneath the abstract
pattern which conveys to the seemingly necessary rational
pattern a note of the whimsical, the arbitrary, a chance-
factor, in other words an element of the absurd. The
petrification may remind of death, the "supreme abuse,"
the "reconciliation with nemesis," expressions used by
Camus and all of them defying the semblance of rational

consistency, a defiance hidden in the very pattern which is presented.

The absurd marriage between necessity and chance is still more obvious in modern music. Stockhausen and Boulez recommend studies in mathematics and engineering. Melody has yielded to discontinuous blocks of sound, rigidly structured but put together at random, and it is left to the performer to decide in which order he wants to play them. This intentional disruption of continuity is a clear declaration of war against life and excludes any kind of development. Because life is continuous and unfolds in a continuous development, modern music has discarded the devices which lead to melody. No melody, no continuity, no development—these destructive principles guide the young composer. Serial music follows instead the mathematical scheme of presenting material for an infinite variety of combinations, and it is the business of combining which delights the musician as a purely intellectual game. Arbitrariness, combined with abstract necessity, chance, and law, substitutes for the representation of life by melody, and so indeed, absurdity has covered up what once had been truth inherent in life.

Are we allowed to detect in all these endeavors something of that absurdity which was hailed in the works of Sartre, Camus, and Kafka? If so, then there may be a serious motivation behind the bewildering structures, behind the destruction of life, behind death. All these deviations may be meant to lead to a new awakening and may be only a transitional stage by which the old is destroyed and must die in order that a new life may be born. That this new life is not yet apparent matters little. Absurdity, wherever it comes to the fore, can only be a storm signal for a new advent. In itself it may well be disturbing, but confidence in the power of life will lead us beyond this phase of mere transition to a truth on which we can rely. The absurdity of destruction and death has a message; poets and artists cry it out to us. We shall not take their saying at its face value, but try to discover what death, destruction, and absurdity hide behind their superficial disguise.

# CHAPTER V

# The Evasive Experience of Death and Its Substitutes

CAMUS AND KAFKA have linked absurdity to death. What they mean, however, is not so much that death as such is absurd, but that the absurdity of life is sublimated and sanctioned by death. This death is not a biological event into which life dissolves; it is a kind of spiritual experience which is present throughout life's course and which conveys a sanction to the meaningless events of life, not the heavy sanction of mythical fate, but the light costume of chance, which dissolves nemesis and corrects our all too serious attitude toward the absurdity of life's process.

Mythology and the philosophy of the absurd supplement each other and meet in the idea of chance. In the mythological realm, our coming and going, birth and death, are equally only chance, although a quasi-necessity is provided by the projection of all these crazy happenings into *illud tempus*, where they receive some kind of necessity. In the philosophy of the absurd, we are again thrown into chance and meaningless adventure, and death is one of these chance-adventures, here without the fateful meaning, a dissolution even of nemesis. But in both cases it is really chance which is in focus, chance either playfully projected into necessity or dissolving necessity. A serious consideration of death is excluded by such attitudes.

But when it comes to death, can we complain about this

treatment? Certainly the attitude toward life is most inadequate in both views. Death, however, is so much at the periphery of life and escapes our experience to such a degree that a playful or absurd treatment is excusable. It must be granted that in modern times there is much talk about death in all quarters, for we have fallen into the habit of using our words loosely and of filling gaps in experience with fiction, which is bare of true insight and vision.

Let us start with the soberest and simplest meaning of death: the biological disintegration of life. What do we know about it? To be sure, we know nothing at all about biological death as far as our own life is concerned. There is no possible approach to it. Freud, in his earlier writings (*Collected Papers*, IV, 305), candidly emphasizes that when we try to think about death, we always do so by imagining ourselves as surviving. In other words, we look at our own death as if it happened to somebody else, on whose death we can therefore reflect as survivors. We split into two people, one of whom is still alive while the other is dead, and this gives us the illusion of experiencing our own death.

Here an objection may be raised: Do we not experience death in the phenomenon of aging, in the weakening of our physical strength? No, we do not. Aging is a process of the living, a certain modification of life as life. In no way does it contain or anticipate the *cessation* of life. It may be a growing impoverishment of life, but it is still life. The cessation of life is in abrupt contrast to the ongoing process of aging and has nothing in common with it. By the way, aging may not be altogether exhaustively explained by considering physical weakening; it may be coupled with a growing spiritual strength and wideness of scope. In any case, it is a complex experience with a processual character. In some people, physical weakening may result in isolation and depression;

in others, it may result in a serenity of the spirit because of the profounder insights, the greater richness of spiritual experience. Both attitudes may even alternate and combine, but never will there be any experience of cessation, of the total annihilation which death alone can mean.

No, we reflect on what we think is death from a very different level. It is similar to our claim of dream-experience, where we reflect on a dream from the platform of fully awakened life and therefore have a distorted view of what may have happened in the dream. The awakened person judging a dream and the living person trying to know about his death, these are indeed absurd and impossible ways of approaching something which is unapproachable, the latter being far more unapproachable than the former.

What remains is thus reflection on another person's death, never on our own. But here we are no better off. Do we really know any more about another person's death than we know about our own? We are obviously the survivors, looking from our own life at the death of another. We cannot possibly enter into the fact of the other's death; we remain in our own favorable position of being fully alive. We may say that the situation of the deceased is totally different from our situation, that his death is "other than life." But this does not mean much. What is "other than life"? We will surely not make the mistake of confusing "other than life" with the inanimate, with situations which have nothing to do with life. Even with regard to inanimate objects we would be at a loss if we wanted to know about their state of being. What is it like to be a stone, a piece of metal, a cloud? With regard to those beings which were once alive, we can merely state that they have ceased to live. But this negative statement does not convey any experience. To be not alive, to be excluded from life, does not reveal any positive knowledge with regard to its status of reality.

We may, however, distinguish between the death of a stranger and that of a person dear to us. The death of a total stranger means nothing, especially if the circumstances of his dying have not been disclosed to us. If the circumstances are known, they may be terrifying and a shock to us. We may identify ourselves with him and in some way experience the agony of his last living moments, but again, this is an experience of life, of a suffering life, not of death. But let us investigate the death of a beloved person. Here the fact that this person is no longer with us colors the experience of our life: our life is impoverished by the loss; there is suddenly a hole in the fabric of our life. We feel a loss, and we experience it as an impact which modifies our life. It is again our life which is at stake, not the death of the other. We the living are impoverished; we the living must adapt ourselves to a new situation which changes our way of existing.

We must return to the death of the beloved, however, and investigate it from another angle. Here we are concerned only with the cessation of life, and such a cessation is not open to any experience whatsoever, whether it is our own or that of others. It is always the survivor, the one who is still living, who reflects on the dead and is, as a living person, excluded from the experience of death.

Let us widen now the scope of our investigation beyond the question of how death as such affects us. Is there perhaps an experience of a spiritual disintegration, akin to the biological fact of death, and do we experience such a spiritual disintegration when threatened by nothingness? It has been claimed in recent times that we are exposed to nothingness, that absolute nothingness confronts man not only at times but perpetually, that we are living in the face of nothingness. I do not think this is true, at least not as an experience of normal man. If psychiatrists insist on the reality of such experiences, it may be that they have come across them in the sickroom among neurotic persons. But the pathological case, as important as it is for the physician, means nothing to the philosopher, who considers man in his maturity and fullness of being. We have the suspicion that when philosophers adopt this attitude toward absolute nothingness, it is the symptom of a time in which a large part of humanity is in a state of neurosis and has been reduced to a primitive bondage. It is this state of bondage and impotence which brings mythological patterns to the fore: fate as a dark foil and setting, and whether this dark foil is called "death" or "nothingness," it is a protective device similar to those devices which mythological man invents in order to escape freedom and responsibility. It is enlightening, therefore, to find, in Heidegger's mythological philosophy, death as the totalizing factor which rounds out life and which is explained as the possibility of impossibility, that is, as the factor which transforms possibilities into impossibilities, projects into something unrealizable, decisions into resignation, freedom into the awareness of captivity, history into a petrification in the narrow circle between birth and death whereby both—and any occurrence between them—seem to be repetitions of the same unavoidable moment, so that life is reduced to a round trip back to where it started, with nothing in between (*Being and Time*, §§ 55, 74). It is this "nothing" which in Heidegger's essay *What Is Metaphysics?* substitutes for death and even for world. Now man is not living toward death or in the world; he is held into nothingness, and this is not meant as a threat but rather—what absurdity meant for Camus—as a dissolution of nemesis, an escape into a night, "a night in which all cows are black," as Hegel labeled Schelling's mythological escape. "Nothing" is an indispensable feature in myth (see p. 13), and it is indispensable in the mythology which has replaced philosophy in modern times.

There is much of Nietzsche's *ressentiment* in this mythology—a transformation of deficiencies, negations, troubles of an uneasy mind into protective schemes, into a frame of seeming strength. Thus unfree, irresponsible man glorifies his unfreedom as a kind of freedom, his lack of future as the destiny of history, his anxiety as care, his inability to make a decision as a special form of resolve with regard to something he cannot possibly influence, his death, his finitude, in the limits of which, however, he feels secure. That "totality" and "possibility" take first place in this philosophy shows that it is not really concrete existence which is here explored but a reflective and abstract view of man, for "totality" and "possibility" belong to the vocabulary of rationalism. "Possibility" as pure and absolute is hailed by some existentialists, although it is the very opposite of concreteness and reality. It is distant to the real and so rather akin to "nothing," substituting for negative freedom, where man remains uninvolved, in the openness of the merely possible. But even relative possibility is abstract, related to an equally abstract necessity of law, whereby the possible is an instance, a possible instance in the structure of law. The real, however, is neither merely possible nor merely necessary but—in the realm, in which alone we can experience it fully—*concrete*, unique, and free. While the possible and the necessary build the structure of science and facilitate our mastering of the inanimate environment, it is in human life and the *communion of person with person* that we experience the concrete, unique reality of freedom. Sartre has turned truth into a lie when he states that man is reduced to a lifeless thing by the look and presence of another person. Hegel came nearer to the truth when he claimed that recognition by another person *gives* meaning and does not deprive of meaning. It is only in the communion of life with life, in the responsibility we take for others, that we receive meaning and destiny. Deprived of this responsibility and communion, we become sick and despair. This is the sadness in the life of old people, cut off from contact with others in a communion of understanding and work. Here life is a "tale told by an idiot," perverted and absurd. This isolation and perversion can be called a "symbolic death"—not death experienced as isolation, but an isolation which can be metaphorically called a kind of death.

Camus has treated the despair of man, cut off from others, in his novels *The Stranger* and *The Fall*, and Tolstoy has given us another example of an isolated and thus wasted life in his novel *The Death of Ivan Ilyich*. Although death is mentioned in Tolstoy's title, it is not death as such which is exposed, but the worthless life, muddled, estranged, and loveless, which is like a death; and when death really approaches, it is only the final seal on the absurd and wasted *life*. Ivan Ilyich feels a gnawing pain as the symptom of impending death, but it vanishes when he feels that there is love in his life, the love of a son and a servant. What Tolstoy wants to say is: Death and its messenger, pain, are the marks of an empty life and a darkened soul. Whether biologically alive or dead, such a person is an absurdity in his desertion. Tolstoy tells us in his *Confessions* that he himself was so depressed by the emptiness of his life that he considered suicide. Emptiness and meaninglessness are death, the only death we can possibly experience.

We should not confuse empty possibility, whether relative or absolute, with the concrete experience of creativity, of power and its free necessity of unfolding. In such a state of unfolding, possibilities may occur as stations of reflection and rest, as obstacles to be overcome—the static will always be subservient to and a way sign on the road of a dynamic

development. The stations of rest may be regarded as ful-
fillments, and a metaphysics may be constructed which debases
the process of life as a mere means, a mere transition to that
in which the process comes to an end, in which the thing is
fulfilled and achievement and goal are the ultimate meaning
to all activity. But such a metaphysics will sooner or later be
abandoned and replaced by its opposite.

# CHAPTER VI

# Life's Process and Its Articulation: Sacrificial Works

METAPHYSICS, the philosophy concerned with the problem of ultimate reality, has in its history turned in alternative stages to answers of an opposite kind. Now it was a fixed, timeless structure of things or ideas, of being as the divine foundation and reality; now it glorified the creative, dynamic, and concrete process of becoming as ultimate and holy and regarded the structure of abstract things as subservient, as merely a potential organization of the process. Plato's reality was a firm, timeless structure of unchanging ideas in a fixed relation to each other. For Aristotle, however, these fixed ideas were drawn into the process of life, were subservient to it, every one a potential reaching beyond itself into the process. Augustine followed this emphasis on a dynamic life, on will—*omnis est voluntas*—and regarded the life-process as ultimate: *vivo ergo sum*. And this remained the attitude of Franciscan philosophy throughout the Middle Ages. On the other hand, it was the Dominican thought of Thomas Aquinas and his school which emphasized a timeless structure of law, of a dogmatic pattern, and although some appreciation was given to Augustinian dynamism, the achievement of things, of works under law, took precedence. Descartes, believing that he was starting on an entirely new road, is an interesting example of the necessary working of history: he manages merely to combine both views. Following

Augustine, he discusses the living process of doubt, of searching—*cogito ergo sum*—but then changes to the metaphysics of things, making God, as well as his own ego, into a thing, a thing which thinks. After Descartes, the split into the former two camps is renewed, with the worshipers of things in one group and the worshipers of process in another. Hobbes will work out a metaphysics of bodies, Berkeley of spiritual power and process, and it will be Kant who wavers again between the two solutions with his activity of apperception and the structure of his categories, the infinite will and the timeless law.

Also in the realm of ethics and religion, emphasis will be either on the process of faith and love or on the works done, the fixed achievements of the process. Whenever the emphasis is on the process of faith and love, fanatics will debase the works, as Luther did, passionately opposed to them as a danger and temptation. A more balanced view will do justice to things and works, recognizing them as potentials on the way, as an articulation of the process, negated somehow and destroyed to make room for the continuation of the process, but while negated and destroyed serving and intensifying the creative process. In this way a highly important discovery will be made: the necessity of sacrifice. Sacrifice will color ethics as well as religion. The works of faith and love are offered as sacrificial objects and will be a challenge and an intensification of the process. To get stuck in things, arrested in works, will indeed be a sin; it will be original sin, fundamentally rooted in human finitude. The problem of original sin is best understood and fits best into reality when seen in this perspective. The glorification of works holds man in the past, arrests him there, and turns him away from the future, which is God's call. He boasts, as St. Paul says, about his achievements, about his fulfilling the structure of law, instead of launching ahead in the dramatic overcoming of all arrests and obstacles, in a conversion from sin to grace. Death is now sin's work; death is in the petrification of things done, boasted about, and possessed. We shall rid ourselves from these traps of death, we shall sacrifice them, for sacrifice is the victory over death—death has its resurrection in the sacramental life. What Nietzsche calls "sublimation" very much later is again the overcoming of arrest by sacrifice, and modern psychology has built on this insight. Who cannot sublimate is caught in death, in sin, and is condemned to a life of repetition and deadly routine.

The transformation of things into potentials of process and its unfolding, into steppingstones, not arresting but fostering life, has supplanted death by sacrifice. We shall not simply discard the structure of things and try to fly into heaven, as the Eastern mystics have done, debasing the world of things as evil or as an illusion; instead, we shall recognize the world, which is neutral, neither good nor bad, but open to both according to our attitude. In Western metaphysics, religion, and ethics, man has acknowledged the value of things, of achievements and structure of law, but has subjected these fixities to a disciplining element which is built into life and its ascending process. We must find our way through the world, with its dangers of arrest; we must, in fear and trembling, work out our salvation. There are periods in which man gets stuck—we mentioned modern abstract art (pp. 26 ff.), which glorifies a fixed pattern of order instead of transcending it by using it as an articulation of life, as a structure of rhythm, subjecting and sacrificing it, enhancing life through triumph over the lifeless pattern.

Thus fixation, petrification, may be regarded as one of the elements in reality, but only an element and only really real when overcome in a sacramental way. Primitive man has understood this and has used death in his initiation rituals, but it was a death which was followed by another life. In a similar way we may look at every finishing, every fulfillment and leave-taking after such fulfillment, as a kind of death, cherished, however, as a sacrificial enhancement of life, which continues. Transmigration may also be mentioned here as a series of deaths, followed by a new life, for which death was merely a stage of necessary transition.

In this sacrificial attitude the element of responsibility is paramount. Man is responsible for the things which he calls his works; he has to make them so that they may serve in the development of not only his own life but also a wider life of which he is a part. In order to do this, he must mold, transform, and partly destroy what comes to him from the past. No work is done in a vacuum, for it always uses what the past has provided, and even though the past is his, an integral element in his life and dear to him, he must transform and destroy, he must sacrifice it for a future that is still unknown and real only in his faith. We must perpetually make and remake ourselves by using our past, by transforming and sacrificing it. In this way—and only in this way—we become what we, ideally, are, and we are compelled by our conscience to do this sacrificial work, because we are called upon to do it, as the meaning of our life.

The powers we regard as our faculties or dispositions are certainly ours, but they are to be developed responsibly, that is, in responding to a call which comes to us from the future and asks us to make the truth in us come true. No development occurs without the sorrow which accompanies the necessity to destroy in order to develop. The child in us, with its charm and innocence, is destroyed in order that the adolescent may appear; the adolescent, with his vivacity and daring, must be sacrificed in order that the masterful adult may be born.

Who tries to escape this sacrificial attitude by preserving and amassing the things of the past will soon be possessed by these his hoarded possessions, petrified and arrested. Who, on the other hand, dismisses the past irreverently and irresponsibly—instead of transforming it in the way in which sacrifice keeps the transformed alive and fruitful—is also arrested, for he has eliminated the ground out of which he could have risen.

Psychologists have assumed that an aggressive instinct is working in man, an instinct to destroy; but what they should have acknowledged instead—and sometimes have—is an inner urge to sacrifice by transforming and to make fruitful that which would be a barrier and an arrest without this sacrificial transformation.

CHAPTER VII

# Sacrifice and Death

WE ARE NOW prepared to enter directly into the positive
character of sacrifice, of the transcendence of life over its
phases, over the danger of arrest. Even Freud acknowledges,
in addition to his "death-instinct," an urge toward union
with other human lives, that is, a tendency to sacrifice
aggressive egoism (*Civilization and Its Discontents*, p. 141). In
literature, men who seem to be filled with the urge for death,
such as Kirillov in Dostoyevsky's *The Possessed* or Chen in
Malraux's *A Man's Fate*, are in reality directed beyond death
toward a sacramental life where annihilation is the door to a
new beginning. The process of life is the indispensable ground
from which the stages of possible arrest receive their character
and meaning as sacrificial deeds or sacramental possibilities.

In other words, not annihilation, not the total destruction
of death, is here intended, but a negation and loss which
points to and finds its meaning in a creative and positive
aspect of life. Sacrifice, even if it is a sacrificial death, is not
an end but a transition to a new beginning. It is an offering
which in its passing away is somehow preserved because it
integrates and intensifies that for which it was an offering. In
the sacrificial deed, that which is seemingly destroyed is made
to live on and is thus not only preserved, but—more than that
—it is elevated and plays a role in a higher sphere of meaning. Here is a destruction which turns into creation; it is an
end which converts into a beginning and has meaning beyond
mere destruction. There is a positive gain in sight which could

only be realized by the sacrificial loss. The eye is directed beyond the loss to a gain, experiences the loss as an element in life itself, an element which is transcended in life's unfolding and receives meaning through transcendence. Only that which is surpassed in our life and imagination can be truly experienced, for it has become part of the life-process. Sacrifice is of this nature, and so too is death when considered as sacrifice. The emphasis of any experienced destruction of life should therefore be on sacrifice; the predominance, however, of the total giving in death has resulted in the mis-understanding that it is destruction as such, as a total end, which is the object of a vital experience. This false attitude must be corrected.

The history of man has suffered in the confusion between death as meaningless destruction and death as a sacrificial and meaningful offering. Instead of the acknowledgment of sacrifice, it was murder which loomed in the foreground. The murder of Abel by Cain, of Remus by Romulus, of Osiris by Set—all of these apparent murders were in fact sacrificial acts which, sanctified by tradition and with the consent of the holy victim, aimed at an intensification of life, the life of the group, the tribe, the family. It is for this reason that Cain became the founder of cities, of culture, and received from God the Cain-mark, not as a sign of abomina-tion, but of divine approval. And both Romulus and Set were regarded as sublime initiators of great cultural periods, of powerful city-life and social advance. It would have been absurd if these men had been plain murderers. But the confu-sion between murder and sacrifice still works in our time, in Freud's theory of an aggressive death-instinct. There is an instinct for sacrificial action in man, for a devotion so strong and pure that it does not even shrink back from giving all and giving what is most dear: life itself.

Now we are at last able to state our fundamental position and finding: what is called the "experience of death" has no reality at all as such, but must be interpreted as the positive and creative experience of sacrifice. Here is not a loss, experienced by the survivor and projected into the deceased, but rather an anticipated gain, constitutive for life itself, a meaning for the sake of which anything whatsoever must yield, including empirical existence as a whole. Man is not, as the philosopher Simmel has put it, "he who is one day to die," for man has this in common with plants and animals. Man is the creature which knows that it has its life for the sake of giving it to a higher fulfillment. Man's life is sacramental. In this way man indeed lives perpetually in the presence of sacrifice and, if it must be, of death. Here is not a necessity, the "when" of which is accidental, but rather a necessarily free decision, experienced in the integration of the whole personality, its past, and its tendencies toward the future. The accidental "when" has vanished in the free decision, which is not a decision to live toward death, but to give everything one has in the present. What was in mythology a dim identity of necessity and chance, developed to absurdity, is here the freedom of decision.

In this way, impersonal, mythological fate is changed into individual, personal destiny. Destiny grows out of man's free decision, and is not, like fate, a rigid determination from above nor a demand from a distant world, throwing man into a problematic status. Destiny belongs to man as *his* destiny, but it is more than merely this; destiny also widens the individual life beyond its confines and makes it reach out into another life with which it is united by this very destiny. Thus the outcome of sacramental attitude will be a communion of life with life. It is true, therefore, that sacrifice, far from isolating man—as was emphasized with regard to death

—frees man from his loneliness and closes him into a living
unity with other people. The absurdity of death lies not only
in its chance-character but also in its supposed isolation,
which renders it meaningless, shutting it off from anything
before and after. Sacrifice, as which alone death can be
experienced, is the very opposite of this empty and isolated
fact; it is devotion, reaching out in giving, and thus it is the
most sublime bond which links life with life. Even when the
sacrifice seems to be made for an ideal or an abstract cause, it
is life itself which, clouded and hidden, calls into the sacrificial
action, a life greater than ours, a life which draws us into our
destiny.

If we now try to understand the experience underlying
the death of the beloved, then we see how far we have moved
away from our former investigation. It is now not death as
the biological disintegration of another person's life, which
indeed could not be experienced at all; what could be experienced was merely the impoverishment of the survivor's
life. But if it is true that sacrifice unites life with life in one
destiny, then the death of the beloved, understood as his
sublime offering, his sacrifice in and for the communion, will
retain the communion between the survivor and the deceased
and will intensify through the sacrificial act the living experience of this communion, in which the deceased, as an offering,
lives on. Far from impoverishing the survivor, the sacrificial
act will enrich him and send him on his way with greater
courage. He will feel strengthened in the permanent presence
of the sacrifice, which has always been the essence of the
loving communion but which has now received its ultimate
seal in the final and total offering: the sacramental nature of
the communion.

The effects of such a sacrificial death are numerous and
contradictory. There will be sorrow because of the removal

of bodily presence, with all the possibilities of care, comfort, and sharing. There will be also a feeling of guilt, because the ultimate sacrifice was a gift which can never be repaid. Guilt is not adequately viewed when it is based on remorse because of insufficient services rendered to the deceased. It is indeed never possible to do enough for a beloved life. But the full awareness of this insufficiency comes to the survivor only through the immensity of the last sacrifice, in the face of which nothing done could ever be sufficient.

But is the death of the beloved really an offering to the survivor? Is such an interpretation not against common sense? It may be against common sense in all those lukewarm communions in which people live side by side rather than in and with each other. But if the communion is, as it should be, a perpetual and unrestrained giving to the other, then the physical exhaustion which marks death is the consequence and the elucidation of the immense efforts the loving life has made for the sake of the other, then death is the ultimate manifestation of the total giving. It has been rightly said that the willingness of husband and wife to give birth to children is a consent to their own death, a sacrificial offering to the coming generation. It is here that death and loving sacrifice are clearly united.

Besides sorrow and guilt, therefore, a deep feeling of gratitude will pervade the heart of the survivor. All that has been done in a lifetime is gathered as in one sheaf in the last offering, in death, revealing once more the fullness and meaning of the life which has departed and the richness of the communion which still continues.

All these feelings contribute to and unite in a renewed call to service on the part of the survivor. His strength of devotion has grown because of the death of his beloved, and he or she will be more intensively aware of the link which binds life to life. For the death of the beloved reveals a last truth to the survivor: behind any communion of love, behind the destiny of the lovers, there is at work a greater life which continues to call into service, an infinitely wide service, not only infinite in time but also infinite in outreach, including all life within our reach. Even the things around us may receive a heightened meaning and may radiate devotion, which has been intensified by the ultimate offering. The tender care which is given to objects, to nature, the dignity all things received in the writings of Rilke and Dostoyevsky, has its reason here. The earth is holy: Raskolnikov and Prince Myshkin both fall down and kiss the soiled earth on which men tread, deeply aware of their intensified service to men.

The free decision of the sacrificial act as the destiny of man has changed self and world. Self is no longer the problem it was, and world is no longer the distant realm into which man reaches only in order to become aware of his deficiency, throwing him into the refuge of mythology, ritual, and magic. World now lives in the communion of mutual devotion and sacrifice, in calling and responding, in free decisions of a responsible nature. Freedom and responsibility belong together, and they are only to be had when man has discovered his sacramental life as his destiny.

It cannot be repeated too often that sacrifice is a conversion from loss into gain, not an end, but a beginning. Only in this its transformation and transcendence can the end, can loss and death, be experienced. We experience only what is built into our life, has become an element in it, and is surpassed by the drive toward future, for life is the drive toward future. If we are arrested in an event, which thus becomes indeed a mere ending with nothing after it, then we are merely the victim of a happening, which does not belong to us, is not ours, but only occurs to us. The meaning of death, experienced as an element of life, is its resurrection out of death. Sacrifice always has its resurrection as its meaning. Such a meaning is not only a possibility with regard to communication but is necessarily communicated, for as such it is a reaching out, a communication to other lives. The absurdity of modern culture, which we discussed in an earlier chapter, has as one of its most conspicuous features the despair of isolation, of impotence with regard to communication between men. Just as no topic is as fashionable today as the experience and fear of death, although this is not an experience but a confusion, so also do writers since Kierkegaard never tire of telling us, with many words, that they are unable to communicate, that all their writing is ultimately a monologue, an intensification of their loneliness. Man's discourse with man, they say, has the one and only effect of throwing him, with greater intensity, back onto himself. This too is a case of absurdity, the absurdity of confusing sacrifice with annihilation, the reaching out to others with being swallowed up by nothingness and isolated in a horizon of darkness. Man, they say, is free only to grasp his being walled in, his imprisonment between two chance-events, birth and death, his fate of being nailed to the cross of an empty ritual of perpetual repetition.

Absurdity, loneliness, death, and isolation are the sinister themes of our time. It is a loquacious outcry of despair for which modern man must blame himself. Since he is unable to experience death as a sacrifice, he should instead be quiet about it, as was Goethe, who never spoke of his son's death, but was somehow aware of his impotence to feel strongly the impact of communion and responsibility. There may have been a similar lack in the life of another genius, Leonardo da Vinci, who was also frigidly separated from his fellow men. In both cases, refuge was sought in the abstract and

impersonal field of science. Although it is not completely satisfactory, such an attitude nevertheless has a positive value:
the inner deficiency is compensated by a service which is not
directly turned toward life but is indirectly devoted to mankind and its future. Science has taken over where man has
lost contact with life—a phenomenon we mentioned in
Chapter IV when we discussed music and art. We find this
same phenomenon in modern care for the aged. It is obvious
that we are more concerned today about emptiness in the
lives of old people than we were in former times. What we
have done, however, is to invent a new science, gerontology,
which is supposed to fill the bill. We hospitalize and institu-
tionalize the aged and hope that this scientific treatment will
reactivate these unfortunate people. But the artificial communion, without the love of family and without the privacy
of the home, will often accelerate the disintegration instead of
stopping it. The timetable takes over, the mere filling of time
by an activity which lacks meaning because it is not born out
of true need, the need to help and to enrich the lives of those
who are dear to us. There is no sacrificial love at work, no
free decision to give oneself, but instead an abstract planning.
Love is replaced by law and order, and so we have fallen into
a cultural development that is diametrically opposed to the
one which, according to St. Paul, Christ introduced. With
Christ, law and order was transformed into love; now love
is transformed into law and order.

Communion and sacrificial love shape the individual's life
and become his destiny, while typification and abstract
planning make love and sacrifice unnecessary, subject man to
the institution, and reduce his life to that kind of frictionless
collaboration which the animal, served by the instincts of
the herd, enjoys. Biologists have rightly stated that man
starts life on a poorer level than the higher animals. He is

more helpless, more reduced than they, as if nature had taken a step backwards. But it is exactly this seeming regression and reduction which has forced the human race to unparalleled efforts: the human individual must go a long way to maturity, but this long way, forced upon him, has given him a dynamic scope that is far superior to anything in the animal realm. While the higher animals merely fructify their bodily potentials, their organs and instincts, and are in direct harmony with their environment, to which their potentials respond, man has had to develop powers to transform and create his own environment. World was thus rising around man in call and response, world in partnership with man, in communion and interaction of person with person, in love and sacrificial devotion, in a truly creative communication between lives.

# CHAPTER VIII

# Mortality

IF MAN EXPERIENCES death at all, it is not that last event in which his life runs out, not biological disintegration. Death as a spiritual experience is perpetually present in the course of our life as a self-sacrifice which converts life by sublimating it. In every essential decision we are taking leave, destroying something of the past, dear and valuable to us, for the sake of a transcendent fulfillment.

We are therefore constantly aware of the inseparable unity between our spatial and temporal existence, on the one hand, and a higher spiritual realm which unfolds in the transformation of that existence. It is not to be wondered that when the idea of a resurrection burst into the biblical mind, it could not be conceived as a mere dropping of the body and rising of the soul alone; the body had to continue to play a role and had to be present at the rise of the soul (Isaiah, 26:19; Daniel 12:2). This was quite a *skandalon* for people educated by Socratic thought, but it grew out of the conviction of a sacrificial transformation and preservation of body by soul, the former having an indispensable part in the sacramental life of the spirit.

This involved a danger, the danger of being arrested in the body and becoming unable to make the sublimation. It was therefore necessary to be ready for the sacrificial act at every moment and to live this readiness, not as a mere possibility which may or may not come about, but as man's destiny, the ultimate meaning of his life. He is rooted in this readiness to give himself totally for something greater, and this is precisely man's mortality.

Mortality is the ever open readiness and presence to a higher sphere. It is an attitude of activity, not a mere passive waiting for a distant possibility. It expresses an actual involvement in a definite future, a reaching out beyond our bodily seclusion. Perhaps Nietzsche divined something of this when he asked man to live dangerously. But there is more involved than danger, than taking risks. He who risks hopes that what he risks may not be taken from him. The readiness for sacrifice hopes nothing of this sort, but regards as the meaning and destiny of its life that the offering will be accepted. Readiness here is neither a mere waiting for a future possible event nor a perpetual involvement in action and adventure. It is a state of tension between past and future, the past gathered up and integrated into a decision which of necessity gives way to free action, to free molding of the future. All of our deeper personality trends are such actual involvements, although they seem to be mere possibilities waiting for realization with the help of still undecided factors of the future. When we call a person "gentle" or, more specifically, "musical" or "mathematically minded" or "gifted with a sense for historical facts," we do not merely describe what may result under certain conditions that are favorable for the realization of such qualities, we mean actual bents, actual commitments, present as facts, a longing and reaching out toward a definite channeling of life.

Thus mortality means the actual presence of a quality, fundamental and meaningful, a responsibility and serious inclination, a perpetual mustering and integrating of all forces in order to have them at the disposal of our destiny. When the philosopher Simmel praises Rembrandt's portraits because they show man with his death, he means not really

death but the mortality inherent in man, the seriousness of
man's readiness to give himself totally and without restraint.
Simmel compares these portraits with pictures of Renaissance man, to whom death comes as an accident from outside,
violently and meaningless. Rembrandt's men know that their
destiny is sacrifice, and this knowledge gives them a seriousness and dignity which is absent in portraits by other artists.

Mortality thus conceived is not passive subjection, but free
and active mastering of death. He who freely chooses his
sacrificial act gives to it its meaning and is its lord. Such a
person deserves our respect, and more than that, our tender
devotion and compassionate love, for his life is burdened with
a tragic responsibility. It will be this tragic element which
will draw our interest in the remaining chapters of this
work.

The feeling which accompanies our mortality is neither
fear nor hope, neither sadness nor joy, and certainly not
resignation. It is the feeling of concentration and intensity,
of tension and crisis. There is no excitement, which comes in
hours of danger and adventure, bolstering up the ego of man
in a sportive way. There is a quiet elation, even a passionate
devotion, in which the loss of the sacrificial act heightens
the awareness of the gain for the sake of which the price was
paid. Whatever feeling may accompany the mortal life,
mortality is a positive, creative status. Its emphasis is not
on limitation, finitude, and negation. This misunderstanding
was only slightly remedied by recognizing a disciplining
quality in such finitude, disciplining because it pointed to the
necessity of economizing with respect to the limited number
of years granted to mortal men. That there is a disciplining
power in mortality is true, but it is not due to a quantitative
limitation of years. Whether our life is long or short is not of
importance; in a short life, often more has been done than in

a long one—we have to think only of Mozart or Schubert. What counts is the qualitative richness of the life, its being spent in sacrificial action at every moment. It may even happen that life is shortened because of a passionate urge to let no opportunity for sacrificial action pass. Nietzsche's life was obviously shortened and his biological disintegration hastened by the immense amount of work he did, by his devotion to his calling. The infinite abundance of life is enhanced by mortality, by the intensive readiness for sacrifice. Mortality thus understood, far from limiting life and expressing its finitude, points to infinity, and the negation in such a life should be recognized as working in the sacrificial destruction which serves a resurrection on a higher plane. Mortality guarantees an infinity of inner richness, an unlimited abundance. It works inside life, not outside, where it would only round out a limited number of years to a finite totality and sum. This kind of limitation and quantitative summing up changes life into a lifeless structure and has no part in the true sacrificial mortality of man, which not only widens every individual life to an infinite destiny, but also, by its sacrificial outreach, links individual life to other and always other lives, guaranteeing in this manner an infinite process of continuation.

It is the latter aspect, so often forgotten, which is most important: that sacrifice tears down the walls between lives and, far from isolating man within the fences of his bodily seclusion, removes loneliness and exposes man to a wide communion. If it is true that readiness for sacrifice, which we called "mortality," is a reaching out beyond the frontiers of the ego, then the decisions made involve us in the lives of others as much as in our own life. Then mortality is a bond between men, a responsibility with regard to others and before others. We live in sacrificial readiness as an infinitely extended interplay of forces, widened beyond any limit and any quantitative negation.

What seems a weakness now becomes a strength, for it makes us concentrate and do our utmost. The qualitative intensification of his sacrificial outreach compels man to superhuman efforts. His unlimited responsibility and destiny makes for a concentration of strength unparalleled by anything before. Death may be received passively, but sacrifice is action and decision and as such it is in need of an integration of power. Will is such an integration and is indeed born out of the qualitative limitation and concentration which sacrifice provides, negating possibilities for the sake of the realization of others. Wishes may preserve an indefinite number of possibilities, indefinite dreams which, hoarded in the soul, remain unrealized and deceive us with the semblance of richness. But no indefinite number of dreams can equal a single realization of the will, which by sacrificing the sterile wish-dreams and the seemingly rich content of life in fact widens the scope of life and the outreach of the doer, allowing him to partake in other lives as in an infinitely extended communion. Passion may work in such a concentration, passion as the awareness of loss; and other apparent deficiencies may contribute, such as poverty, sickness, the trial of suffering and even of impending death. But all of these experiences change, in the light of sacrifice, from loss into gain. Thomas Mann has pointed to the creative element in sickness, made aware of it by Nietzsche's tragic destiny. But here caution is necessary. Such experiences are ambivalent; they may enrich, but they may also impoverish. The sickness of Job proved creative, and so did the sickness of a Dostoyevsky. Wealth, which the Bible accuses of being an inducement to indolence, may be an inspiration for service, for stewardship. But no absolute necessity is to be relied upon. All these facets of life can lead to destruction as well as to an ascent. The only important and reliable feature is readiness for sacrifice, which we called "mortality." If mortality is present and vivid, then all those experiences we mentioned will become contributions, blessings, even sickness and death.

The conversion which lies at the bottom of the phenomenon "mortality" as a concentration on sacrificial destruction, changing over into a creative expansion, makes mortality shine in the light of a beyond which rises out of the surrender to death and survives in the intensification of that very life which was given. It is the "more than mortal," the "non-mortal," the "immortal," which rises at the horizon of mortality. What we thus express in negative terms assumes a negative character only because it must be understood in the perspective of its opposite, because it is experienced in its opposition—the immortal from the perspective of mortality, the infinite from the perspective of finitude. Infinity, immortality, innocence—all of these negations express true experiences, not vague ideas, dreams, or abstractions, but experiences concretely approached from their opposites. Thus mortality must be understood as a transition from death to something beyond death, an intensified state of existence in which that which has been surrendered is preserved, strengthened, sublimated, and widened beyond its finitude into a kind of immortality. Mortality, far from fencing man into his bodily isolation, opens up into the realm of the immortal, and it is at the peak of our mortal life that we are fully aware of this widening, while in childhood and in the senility of old age mortality is hidden to us and the sacramental expansion is reduced to the narrow circle between birth and death. Here a dark fringe surrounds our life, a nothingness into which we are held and which isolates us from our fellow men, making us irresponsible and depriving us of the unifying experience which service provides.

The widening of life, the resurrection from sacrifice, the immortal, seen in the perspective of mortality, is what we may call the "realm of value" (see Chapter X). Value is not a mere possibility nor is it a necessity, both of which are abstract, relative, reflective, and belong to the spatial and temporal level. Value is concrete and absolute and can be regarded as infinite because of its categorical and all-embracing character. The sacrificial act in space and time opens up toward the absolute and infinite value-sphere as the fulfillment and ultimate meaning of that which passes away. Thus immortality as the perspective of mortal, sacramental life assumes the reality of value, and it is in this concrete realm of value that lives meet and that destiny resides, reaching down into our temporal existence as a claim upon mortal man. To regard value as either nonexistent, as Heidegger did in his major writings, or as merely negative, as we find it in Sartre, is a misunderstanding which removes the creative and inspirational element from life's unfolding.

Mortality as a perspective toward the immortal value-sphere should be used only for human existence. Neither plants nor animals are mortals. They simply perish. They do not sacrifice themselves for a higher realm in which they participate. They are subjected to the necessity of biological law and are possible instances of this necessity. Human readiness for sacrifice is therefore not to be conceived as a possibility with regard to the necessity of a future realization, but as a present commitment to that ever present and ever future realm of value.

The ambivalence of mythical man, who, tossed around in chance-possibilities, seeks shelter under the ruling necessity of fate, has given way to a sacramental life of free, responsible,

and ever present decision beyond possibility and necessity.
But such a free decision is indeed open to desertion, to an
escape from sacrifice. Desertion, however, is not fundamental
for human existence. Here enters the mode of possibility. It is
a possibility that man deserts his sacrificial destiny, and this
may undermine the dynamic working of a concentrated life.
The possibility of desertion, of escape from responsibility
and sacrifice, is always with weak man. His bodily enclosure
may be a bridge to a sacramental life, it may lend itself to the
offering which lifts man beyond himself, but this same body
may arrest man in his limitation and deficiency. He may become possessed by his body instead of transcending its
arresting barriers. He may even enjoy his deficiency and
arrest in the possession of his static bodily enclosure and
become proud of it as well as of other bodily possessions and
static achievements. This is the ever present temptation to
which man is exposed, and the tempter may be mythically
pictured as the serpent in Paradise or as Satan. But the
tempter may also be a friend, a disciple, as Peter was to
Christ when he tempted Him to avoid sacrifice and desert
His sublime destiny. It was because of this temptation that
Christ called Peter "Satan."

It may happen that we rationalize our desertion in order to
justify it before our conscience, and this may be done by
erecting before us the protecting screen of projects, systematized and given a semblance of necessity, to which we submit
as if this were our true destiny. But it is only a screen
behind which to relax. Projects may become part and parcel
of our sacramental service, and then indeed do they justify,
for they lead into sacrifice, not away from it, as steppingstones to a life of value and destiny.

Emphasis on a rational, static, self-fulfilled structure as an
interrelated system of totality has, in the history of man's

failures, substituted for reality and has, as the "ideal of perfection," of "perfect, total being," become the object of divine veneration. It became the pagan divinity from Parmenides through the time of Plato and after. Self-sufficient and self-enjoyed, it was enthroned as the model for human life, which now stood alone in its self-sufficiency and self-enjoyment, ruling out any sacramental action and depriving man of his readiness for sacrifice, his true destiny, his sublime mortality. Biblical man had to restore sacrifice and again humble man in that mortality which rules over the individual as his personal destiny, channeling his life, cutting out what does not serve, sacrificing what is dear in order that man may serve. Serving, not being, is the ultimate concern, serving, reaching into the future as destiny and reaching into other lives in a dynamic directedness which presupposes a constant offering and sacrificing. To be sure, man has reduced his life; in order to realize his direction, he must either destroy or diminish the number of possibilities of being. We may here speak of life's reduction to a "role," if we are aware that "role" means, not an insincere adoption of a transitional attitude, but an honest and perpetual channeling of action into a certain reduced pattern. It is characteristic of Greek thought that it symbolized role with a petrified artificial screen, a mask. The mask, worn on stage by the tragic hero, was the archaic residue of an older tradition which regarded personality and its task as a diminution of being, as something inferior. The word *persona* even meant, originally, this very mask, worn for dramatic purposes. We may regard Greek tragedy as the medium for a rebellious new truth, the truth of life *versus* lifeless being, but the traditional mask pointed back to a culture in which the *persona* was a negligible entity, seen in the light of an unchanging and sublime fate, crushing life with its iron and lifeless necessity.

Even in our day thinkers slip into pagan contempt for the role. Sartre, a most brilliant but at times cynical thinker, emphasizes the importance of the role, but he regards role as a symptom of bad faith and points to the fact that we exaggerate our role because we enjoy hiding behind it, just as the Greek actor hid behind his mask. It cannot be denied that this happens and that at times people use the role for the sake of dishonesty, a play, an unserious adoption of a superficial screen. But what we have to consider is that the role, as a task, becomes the channeling of our strength into a definite direction and that, thus understood, the role is man's way of reaching out beyond the confines of his life into other lives under destiny. Here we do not *play* a role but *are* the role; we have reduced ourselves to the role, have sacrificed many possibilities dear to us for the sake of realizing the channeled activity of our role. The decision we make as young persons about our vocation, our calling, is made in clear awareness of resignation with regard to other activities we love and would like to adopt, and so sorrow may overcome us, but courage and faith keep us in our adopted role as a road to service.

Our mortality as a perpetual readiness for sacrifice is thus expressed in our role, and the price paid by sacrifice will intensify our strength to carry out the demands of this very role.

And now we may close this chapter by pointing to the fact that just as mortality was not a mere possibility with regard to future death but the ever present involvement in sacrifice, so too is our total corporal status, our embodiment in space and time, more than just this—it is a means to transcendence, a concrete and present bridge to spiritual fulfillment. We live our body as a perpetual conversion of the body into spirit. Christians have made this very clear by referring to their God as "incarnate." Incarnation means more than the word "embodiment" suggests; it means embodiment with the perspective of annihilation, of the Cross and the Resurrection. The Crucifixion is not an event added to the Incarnation as a possibility only, nor is the Resurrection such a possible afterthought. The incarnation of Christ means Cross and Resurrection as inherent in the Incarnation. When we expand this thought to include the human sphere, we become aware that we too are incarnated, that we are given bodily status for the sacramental rising, that the limiting of our role in space and time is already surrender, devotion to sacrificial transformation. The Christian message should contain the philosophical truth about man as such and should be allowed to extend into the life of every human creature. Just as it is no accident in the life of Jesus, the Christ, that, as incarnated, He met with His death and its resurrection, so too is the destiny of every human being not an accidental offering but essentially his mortality, with a perspective directed toward spiritual sublimation.

# CHAPTER IX

# Sacrifice and the
# Tragic Element in Life

IF WHAT WE said in the preceding chapters is true, that life in
its core is a perpetual conversion from a lower sphere to a
higher one, destroying the lower for the sake of realizing the
higher, then this creative destruction, this sacrificial action,
conveys to life its essential character, which is sacramental.
It can be called "tragic." Life in its maturity is a tragic
drama because it cannot be lived without the perpetual
destruction of that which is dear to us. For whether the
object of destruction and sacrifice is corporal and sensuous
or whether it is mental—our past memories and achievements
—it is always a part of ourselves which we must sacrifice, it is
always self-sacrifice, and thus it is accompanied by sorrow
and suffering. This is all the more so when self-sacrifice carries over into other lives near and dear to us, lives which are
hurt by the sacrificial destruction, drawn into it, thus adding
to our sorrow.

Sorrowful destruction is inevitable: man is under necessity
to destroy what is his own and dear to him, and this will have
ramifications in other lives. Although inevitable, necessity
will have the character of a free decision, a dictate of the
doer's destiny. Man can desert his destiny and escape into a
shallow security, as we have mentioned and as was done on a
large scale with the help of the mythological setting, but in
doing so he will lose his freedom, his individual uniqueness,

his true personality under destiny. True personality should not, however, be identified with man's psyche as it functions and is observed in the mechanism of motivation. The urge for sacrifice and its reaching out for a realization beyond the narrow confines of the ego are not fully explainable by psychological, typical, and rational motivation. On the contrary, psychological motivation may instead explain man's desertion of sacrifice and escape from destiny, his resistance, his arrest in achievements and the proud self-confirmation they provide. The drive toward sacrifice and the realization of a higher value have their roots in a deeper soil, to which sacrifice points. The narrow confines of the observable psyche lend themselves to scientific exploration and to laws of determination. In the crisis of his sacrificial outreach, however, man knows himself to be free, free for his destiny, which grounds him in a more comprehensive and more complex sphere than his little ego would have been able to provide.

This is a highly paradoxical situation. Rationalization has tried to simplify and reduce the paradox by concentrating on ego-motivation only, emphasizing either determination by environment as unfree or the character of the ego as free. But the disturbing truth is that free decision is motivated by a wider necessity, by a destiny which without destroying the freedom of the individual modifies it and gives it the tragic character it possesses. What happens because of environmental circumstances or as the outcome of the doer's character is never tragic. It may be sad. Sad is the destruction of a life in an automobile accident; sad is the loss which results from deficiencies in the character or the intelligence of the loser. Most court cases lack tragedy, as do most events of our daily life. They are simply sad. Only when loss or destruction result from a free decision, a sacrificial act, and at the same time reveal a necessity of more than psychological nature, a necessity of destiny, only then are we allowed to speak of a tragic event.

What, after all, is this mysterious destiny which without removing the freedom of the doer cannot be fully explained by psychic motivation? Destiny is somehow beyond the person who acts under destiny. But destiny is also intrinsically united to the doer, *his* destiny. When we regard man as acting under destiny, we emphasize the fact that man's decision transcends the mechanism of psychological motivation: man is here called into his decision as a decision of sacrifice by a greater power. The doer may not at every moment feel the impact of that greater power; he may at times be dazed by the immediate effects of his doing and deceive himself into believing that this is all that is at stake. But sooner or later it will dawn upon him that his psychological motivations fall sadly short and are themselves meaningless when not lifted into the sphere from which the call came, so that his doings receive a sacrificial value, not directly intended, but ultimately responsible for what happened under destiny.

If we try to name the mysterious realm from which the call of sacrifice comes, this destiny, then we should be aware that any name will be inadequate and will somehow only point to the mysterious source from which the call originated. We may speak of the "communion of lives," of which the doer is a member (see p. 45), but not in the social sense of a rational and utilitarian setting. It would be rather a communion of forces in which the person of the doer is involved with all his being, not just in certain regards and for the sake of limited interests. Such a communion of total and unlimited sharing is a communion of love or friendship, absolute and unique, unaffected by the ups and downs of everyday life, holier than any single life but conveying dignity to the life which serves in it, responsible for the wider life of communion. Thus the call of destiny comes from an extended reality, a wider self than the individual, but from a reality of which the individual is a constitutive member. He is ruled by it, forced not from outside but from within by his own participation in the ruling power, which, calling him, leaves him free, autonomous, responsible but guided, drawn forward by the calling power. It is because of this that the doer says "yes" to his destiny, even when it destroys him or at least involves him in suffering.

The free necessity of sacrifice as it responds to the call of destiny is tragic. We can now understand that tragic sacrifice is not exhaustively explained by the needs and motivations of the doer himself. But it would be a grave error to explain these happenings by means of environmental chance-events. Although they are not fully predictable, they are by no means accidental. On the contrary, their unpredictability has its roots in the opposite pole from chance. Chance is an isolated and thus meaningless fact, but here unpredictability results from so wide a context, from such a complex unity of facts, that a simple derivation is impossible. That there is a meaningful unity of influence, however, is experienced in the tension, the suspense, with which doer and spectator receive the unpredictable course of events. Both doer and spectator live the unshakable belief that there is a meaningful power and that it will reveal itself at the end. In early tragedy the suspense was resolved by surprise, abruptly and as if originating from a distant source, so that a chance-interpretation with regard to the doer was not quite unjustified. But the more tragedy matured, the less the chance-element appeared, being foreign to destiny and the tragic.

The tragic event not only surpasses the scope of individual motivation and individual needs but also surpasses, in its effects, the individual life of the doer and reaches into all of those lives which share the communion and hence the destiny of the hero. The hero's sacrificial act draws the other lives into sacrificial suffering; they too will be afflicted by loss and may even perish. The profound interaction and unity of self with other selves is nowhere so obvious and of such intensity as in the tragic and sacrificial response of man to the call which comes to him from this very unity and communion. On this level, self-sacrifice always means the sacrifice of the wider self, the self of communion, whereby a total giving is at stake. Whether we sacrifice certain possessions or the treasures of the past, these objects will reach deeply into the life of man and will even affect, hurt, and sadden others, those who are near and dear to us, our parents and our friends, all of whom glory with us in our memories and past achievements.

On the other hand, sacrifice intensifies and enriches life. It is the price paid for our growing future and strength. Intensification too surpasses our ego and radiates into the life of communion, sanctifying this wider life by means of the sacrificial act. Therefore, the doer knows that what he does makes him responsible for other lives, with regard to the good as well as to the bad. Responsibility is tightly united with the tragic sacrifice; the free decision carries with it free responsibility. The doer may not always be fully aware of the scope of this responsibility, but a prophetic vision will open to him the knowledge that what has risen out of a wider life embraces and reaches the communion of lives which are his destiny. In a way, he is only the instrument of this wider communion of lives.

What we have tried to elucidate is not so much the poetic content of tragedy, but the tragic element in man's life as it unfolds every day. Although this is the case, the tragic crises of every life are no different from those which, in an intensified and condensed form, are displayed in the tragic drama of the poetic genius. The poet merely uncovers for us that which was veiled and often distorted and watered down in everyday life by the drab of daily routine. Not everybody is a hero, but everybody is a man under destiny, unless he is a deserter. It is a mistake to regard poetry as totally divorced from daily life. Poetry is this very life, but purified, so that the depth of human nature comes clearly to the fore, and this depth is sacrificial service to the wider and all-comprehensive life of communion.

Here we must try to gain a better understanding of Aristotle's view with regard to tragedy than is generally secured. Aristotle speaks of an "erring" on the part of the hero (ἁμαρτία [fault], *Poetics*, 1453a10), and it is usually understood that the erring involves the hero in his tragic destiny. This is not altogether wrong, but it must be supplemented by another aspect of Aristotelian aesthetics: the belief that the character (ἦθος) of the hero is not as important as the integrated story (μῦθος). If this is so, then the character-erring is not decisive, for decisive is that wider pattern which is called μῦθος. What does Aristotle mean by μῦθος? Surely not the myth, discussed in Chapter III of this essay, nor the plot as a mere sequence of events. No, this sequence has a tight inner unity, relying not so much on the character of the hero and his erring as on that metaphysical structure which is the truth in man's life, his πρᾶξις (action, total conduct; 1450a16–20 of the *Poetics* and also discussed in the *Nicomachean Ethics*). It is the whole integrated life: "One swallow does not make a spring" (*Nicomachean Ethics*, 1098a18). It is not a measurable quantitative whole, however, but is manifested in the great moments of life, in the unshakable stability of mature man, in the deeper meaning of his existence (*Nicomachean Ethics*, 1100b18). The character, the ethos of man, is only like a contributing coloring in a picture (*Poetics*, 1450a18, 1451b1), but the integrated πρᾶξις is the true meaning of man's comprehensive life (*Poetics*, 1450a38). This πρᾶξις, therefore, is very similar to what we called "destiny," the pattern raised above the character and defying rational motivation, the wider self of a man under destiny. Here the nobility of the hero, emphasized by Aristotle, has its seat, and it is nobility rather than the mere erring of the subordinated character which is the source of tragic destruction. Thus understood, Aristotle's view on tragedy rightly emphasizes, in addition to the psychological error of character, the wider setting of the mysterious πρᾶξις as a superempirical and decisive structure of the heroic life.

It is, therefore, a pedestrian outlook which registers with moral satisfaction the final downfall of tragic man as if it were punishment for some kind of guilt. There may be guilt present, and so it is understandable that we are inadvertently drawn into a moral judgment. The friends of Job did exactly this and were rebuked by Jehovah for doing it. They missed the tragedy in Job's life. We must face the necessity of destiny, which, without acquitting, does not ask for moral retribution but carries us, together with the tragic doer, beyond suffering and despair into destiny as an extended sphere of life, including many neighboring lives, which were hurt, as the doer was, but which were also heightened in intensity and richness by that very act of the sacrificial sufferer, so that we can, with the sufferer, say "yes" to his downfall. In the story of Job, the intensification is narrated naïvely as a restoration of the loss. But it is more than that; it is the lifting, by means of sacrifice and destruction, into a higher realm.

Death has usurped quite undeservedly the predominant role of the sacrificial act. It is true, sacrificial death shows clearly that sacrifice has an impact on *other* lives, for death as sacrifice can only be experienced in its influence on the survivors, intensifying and giving a heightened meaning to their future years. Thus death as sacrifice is received as an immense gift and leaves the receiver in gratitude to a holy event which re-creates his life. The poet Rilke could speak in this context of death as the "fruit of life," as an event the meaning of which is birth (*The Book of Hours*, pp. 120 ff.). But as much as this form of sacrifice points to the heightened effect on other people's lives, united in a communion of destiny, it falsifies the nature of sacrifice by one-sidedly considering the gain in the other lives and discarding the elation of the sacrificial life *itself*. Therefore, a more representative form of self-sacrifice is to be found in those acts which in the course of a life make that life richer through sacrificial offerings. In such cases the doer will manifest the heightening of his life by his intensively purified emotions. He will, of course, show sorrow, tension, and suspense, will be bewildered by the unpredictable course of destiny; but he will also rejoice in faith, in a new certainty, in an intensity of love and service, when the meaning of his sacrifice fully dawns upon him.

Even when death occurs, it is not the only, not even the decisive, sacrificial act; it is rather only the final seal on the sacrificial destruction which has preceded, leaving the hero in that disturbed but at the same time intensified state of existence which is the result of a sacrifice during life itself. Thus Oedipus' killing of his father is the tragic act resulting in the suffering of the hero after his deed has been revealed to him, while the death or disappearance of Oedipus is only the ultimate seal after years of suffering have purified him. The passionate destruction of Desdemona by Othello is the tragic act under destiny, and the terrible remorse is the impact on

the hero's life, his final suicide only the seal. Similarly is
Macbeth's derangement the working of the tragic destruction
in him, while his death is merely the outward realization of
his inner death, which, however, is also his redemption and
purification. King Lear's tragic sacrifice is his slowly develop-
ing free decision, under destiny, to cast off pride and kingly
glory to become naked, a fool tossed around in storm and
night, but at the same time it exposes him to the hidden powers
of love, in which he is struck by his daughter's death so that
he too succumbs at the end. It is because death is here obviously only a seal of purification during life that some critics
proposed to have a purified Lear live on with his daughter.

Besides passion, there is quiet satisfaction in the tragic
event as it impresses the spectator, but there is no anxiety,
and neither is there the resignation which myth provides.
There is conflict in the happenings which lead to destruction,
but the readiness for sacrifice has overcome this conflict,
has resolved it in the free offering under destiny.

Man certainly lives as a citizen of two worlds, but there is
really no conflict between these two worlds, the one being an
indispensable condition for the other, serving and inspired by
giving itself to sacrifice in order to realize the higher world of
an intensified and more abundant life. Plato and the Far
East have indeed erected a wall between the two worlds and
have debased the one as evil or as a mere illusion, standing in
the way of the other, in conflict with it. Socrates and the
Indian arhat eliminate the spatial and temporal world in
order to rejoice fully in the world of salvation. No tragic view
is present here; neither is the Platonic Socrates a tragic
figure, nor is Buddha. They simply rise to the only reality
there is for them and dismiss what is meaningless anyhow.
There is no sacrifice and no suffering, but simply enlightenment, the transcendence of an illusionary realm in which the

body was tossed around, a trivial disorder which the saved man is happy to leave behind. It is not to be wondered that Plato condemned tragedy and its wisdom and fought violently against its adoption. There is in this Greek and Indian enlightenment an estrangement from the sacramental life and destiny of the individual, from the unique personality and its inevitable perspective to its destiny. Only Aristotle had an insight into the sacramental life, which biblical wisdom had discovered and cherished long before. Thus Aristotle rightly became the philosopher of the religious biblical Middle Ages. His analysis of the Greek tragedy may not satisfy us in every point, but it is surely conceived from a deep admiration for its spiritual nature.

The tragic element, grounded in the sacramental life of man, is indeed the main theme of the Bible as far as human life is concerned. It dawned upon biblical man in early times that self-sacrifice is the core of his existence and that it effects and elevates a wide communion of lives. Man is elected for suffering, for sacrifice, for a trial, not for his own sake, but for the sake of a wide communion of lives. This is man's destiny, and only by this destiny is sadness transformed into sublimation of the tragic. Man is responsible for mankind and is in this way representative, not in the abstract scientific and symbolic way by which Greek rationalism conceived of man as a representative of the species. Responsible for those he loves, man draws them into his tragic and sacramental life. Thus Abraham was called to self-sacrifice by surrendering his only son. Jacob was called to a struggle with a higher power which left him mutilated but blessed in his offspring. Moses was called to the sacrifice of forty years' suffering in the desert, only to die before reaching the Promised Land, but making arrival possible for his people through his sacrificial life and death. The "suffering servant" of the second Isaiah in the sixth century B.C. is a most glorious example of tragic sacrifice and elation that is ultimately fulfilled in the Cross of Christ and man's purification by the messianic intercession.

But here a desperate question may arise, the question which Job put to God: Why must there be sacrifice and suffering, the destruction of that which is dear? Would it not be sufficient if that which must be destroyed were fit for this destruction and abandoned without sorrow? Are Socrates and Buddha not more enviable models for men than Job and the prophets of Israel? No, they are not. The wholesale degradation of life, its diminution to illusion and irreality, makes it indeed easy to rise above without sorrow. But the realm risen to is an empty nirvana and expands its emptiness into life down here on earth. With the abandonment of sacrifice and sorrow, the value of life and of man vanishes too. We have to maintain the fundamental importance of sacrifice in human life as a creative element of utmost importance.

# CHAPTER X

# Inspiration and Value

IN SACRIFICE we have found the solution to our problem. We had to discard the false experience of death, of total destruction, of absolute annihilation in nothingness, and we were compelled to rely upon the sacramental life, where destruction results in creation, where loss is fulfilled in gain. Indeed, this experience was behind all of the various shades of absurd and distorted pseudo-experiences from which man escaped into myth, ritual, and magic, as modern poets and painters have done, or into quasi-scientific structures worshiped by avant-garde musicians. Man is here isolated and wrapped up in his frenetic endeavor to escape his anxiety, finding shelter against the unpredictable unfolding and richness of life.

When sacrifice entered the scene, a light broke through the darkness; absurdity gave way to meaning, and life was rediscovered when used as a gracious gift, a precious offering. Mortality became readiness for sacrifice, and sacrifice assumed a wider meaning in destiny. Life was sacramental and tragic, for it was an offering for something beyond ourselves.

This analysis is not complete, however, unless we manage to divorce, once and for all, the sublime sacrifice from the various utilitarian activities by which something is given away for the sake of greater profit. Utility is indeed behind all those acts which as means point to a purpose. Means and purposes share a rational relationship with utility. But this is not true of sacrifice; it is never a means for profit, never an expense incurred for some gain. There is a fundamental inadequacy between the act and its meaning, for the meaning belongs to an absolute realm which is beyond the realm of relative and spatio-temporal action. The sacrificial act is a finite occurrence, but that for which it is done is beyond space and time, and we therefore call it the infinite, absolute, and eternal "realm of value." Value is not purpose, as was believed by Kant, who spoke of an "absolute end," a "purpose with all." Ends and purposes are relative and are not different in character from their means; they even turn out as means for further purposes.

We should discard in this context not only the idea of purposes but also that of their means. It is true that while value is beyond our making and is instead open to discovery only, the sacrificial act is our doing and seems to be subjected to our arbitrary *choice*. This was what Aristotle believed when he regarded the τέλος (end) as beyond choice but the means which led to it as exposed to our pondering and selecting. Although the sacrificial act is our doing in space and time, it is dictated by value, by our faith in value, which uses our capacity of mastering environmental facts but which hits only those facts which in the light of faith and value are apt to bring value into existence. We may speak here of "inspiration" rather than rational choice, a necessity of a very special character which addresses itself to the whole person, to the self, and asks for the giving of self in whatever form it is demanded. There is a mystery surrounding the giving, a more than rational or utilitarian choice, and it is because of this mysterious element that an event not fully understandable, such as death, will be a preferred object of sacrifice for the realization of value. It is because of this that here, unlike the choosing and pondering of means, no hesitancy, no doubt, will interfere.

The realization of value by sacrifice will proceed under firm inspiration; decision, although free, will not open to choice. No utilitarian motivations will be sufficient; not even motivations like honor or glamor will have a place here. The ego and its narrow psyche are transcended, because destiny is turned to a wider life of responsibility and service (we shall discuss this point in the next chapter, which deals with intercession). Sorrow and agony, love and compassion will be present, but they will not motivate; they will simply accompany and color the sacramental act. The lack of motivation, of causal relation between the act and its sphere of fulfillment, will be understood if we consider that the act as such is rooted in the individual life, while its meaning and direction are raised beyond the individual and comprehend the wider life of value and destiny. Since the volume of the wider life is indeterminate and may even be growing in the action of the doer, it cannot in any way have a fixed causal nature and determine the act.

It is a misuse of language to speak in such cases in a teleological manner, pointing to a purpose in its abstract fixation. In tragic drama, where sacrifice is the fundamental issue, the rational purpose lacks conviction. Antigone's action is not exhaustively explained by sisterly love, nor is Macbeth's tragic doing caused simply by ambition. It was a wider meaning of destiny which inspired these tragic heroes and ended in agony and destruction. It seems at times as if the hero withdraws from his narrow environment and reaches out for a wider human circle. Antigone seems to forget her betrothed, and Hamlet seems cruelly to neglect his love, Ophelia. In reality, however, all these lives, and more, are included and participate in the sacramental offering, and the semblance of a withdrawal was only meant as an attempt to take a wider, all-embracing interest in the surrounding world. Responsibility and scope of action have reached such dimensions and are lifted into such height and distance that all nearness is swallowed up and immersed in the vaster realm.

When we are faced with inspiration instead of mere motivation, we may speak of "genius," and we may use this word specifically with regard to those sacrificial acts which create a value that is obviously unexplainable by what went into the doing of the creator. Also, the words "creator" and "creation," instead of "maker" and "making," point to a mysterious inadequacy between the invented construction and its higher meaning, the value of beauty. Here we have intentionally widened the scope of the sacramental offering and have included both the hero in the tragedy and its author. We may think that we must completely divorce the author from his work, that the tragic poet may offer us in his work an act of sacrifice while he himself remains aloof, but this would be a misconception. The poet would be unable to depict such a life vividly and convincingly if he were not involved in it. The creation of a great work of art is a sacrificial act, and thus we experience the same inadequacy between the structuring and inventing aspect on the one hand and the value of meaning on the other. It is this inadequacy which may fall as a shadow upon the life of the creative person and which would at times cause him to lose direction if inspiration, a light from the value-sphere, did not pierce the darkness and transform his life, in spite of perpetual agony, into a blessed one. The bodily, material, spatio-temporal, and sensuous structure must ever be built and must ever be transcended by sacrificing it for the sake of a dimly conceived value received in faith. Creation is not "out of nothing"— *creatio ex nihilo*—but it reduces to nothing the very structure which it has built in order that the value of beauty may come into being. Thus the structuring is not a means for a purpose, and we do not receive the work as we understand its purpose; it is, as a result of inspiration, a sacrificial act, and we enter this inspiration and sacrificial act, share in it, and thus become participants in the higher realm of value.

Here we are faced with a profounder understanding of freedom. Freedom cannot be subjection to any purpose, but is to be found in inspiration by value, and such inspiration drives a person unhesitatingly and indubitably toward action. Inspired decision is not exposed to or a result of choosing. There is no freedom in choice, where man wavers and hesitates uneasily and feels an imposition and necessity to choose. Detached from his utilitarian self and all petty considerations, man is lifted out of his natural situation by inspiration so that he can give himself freely. His natural situation is freely molded according to the inspiring value, which has been discovered and raised above his life. Thus divorced from his past and the pressure of his narrow present, the free person will enter into the creative sphere, and if the inspiration came from another life and its value, he will enter into that life as a beloved life; he will not only understand and serve it but will free it from its environmental pressure. Responsibility will be linked to freedom, responsibility for carrying out the realization of the value, even if this means turning against environment and success. The free person may not only have to sacrifice his own security and success, but may be compelled to do the same with regard to those lives for which he takes responsibility. He will have to risk and to hurt in order to fulfill his responsibility in the higher realm. Distance to the interests of his ego, as well as to the interests of others who are near and dear, will be a severe duty involving suffering and sacrifice. This was the experience of the biblical prophets and is the prophetic experience of all men under the impact of value.

It is understandable that in times of weak faith the sacrificial action does not occur. Now the activity which should be inspired by value and should be an offering to value remains in its own sphere of sensuous and intellectual procedure, finding meaning, if at all, in the mere continuation of its performance and on the level of this performance. Here no sacrifice is asked; the profound seriousness of the act is discarded. It is in modern art, poetry, and music, yes, even in modern philosophy, that devotion is replaced by activity for its own sake. A Sartre glories in the infinite ongoing of life's activity as a perpetual destruction of itself, with no transcendence and with only a semblance of values, created in the process and discarded in the process. Jaspers similarly worships life, in which agony and shipwreck throw man back into the process, whereby a seeming transcendence renews the process by its perpetual disintegration.

This modern attitude undoubtedly reveals an admirable dynamism which has entered modern art, music, and drama and is far superior to the static structure of ritual, magic, and absurdity in which art was caught some time before and which we discussed in Chapter IV. There is openness, risk, adventure, but what is not yet present—or is only blurred— is the rise to value and destiny, because the lack of faith, sacrifice, and devotion makes this ultimate creation impossible. It is characteristic of modern thinking that the wider self which we mentioned in Chapter IV, the self of communion and love, is clouded or totally absent. Heidegger (*Being and Time*, § 26) limits man's *Mitsein* (being together) with others to the "unauthentic life" of superficial curiosity and small talk, while authentic man is fenced in by his unsharable death; Jaspers regards communication as valuable only for the intensification of the ego, for that ongoing process of life without real transcendence; Sartre takes a more complex attitude, for he regards our fellow creatures as constitutive and invests even God with the task of being an ever present onlooker at our side; but all of this is rather damaging, an unavoidable danger in man's existence, a regrettable facet of life, not a creative element to be gratefully accepted.

Thus the meaning of sacrifice in a wider sphere of value finds little nourishment, and we would therefore expect only a rudimentary art, poetry, and music, perhaps something on the level of a dynamic self-expression of life, of power. However, it is to be noted with gratitude, as a silver lining at the horizon, that an outspoken emphasis on communion, on cooperation, has entered the art and music and poetry of the youngest generation. It is as if these people turn away from the proud isolation of faithless man with a vengeance and humbly resign any fully separate activity of their own. Although they are still only groping their way and have not found faith in a clearly conceived value—so that their activity is at times playful and slightly trivial—their teamwork suggests that there is something beyond the lonely individual, something which only an action for and with others can provide. What I have in mind is that group which allows the composer or playwright only to make a suggestion, which is to be completed by another mind, by the musical performer or the dramatic actor. There are dramatists, like Beckett or Pinter, who provide a sketch for the actor and leave it to him to give full meaning to their work. If it is true that Beckett refuses to give a strict answer to the question of whether *Waiting for Godot* means *Waiting for God* and if Pinter leaves open the problem of whether, in his *Caretaker*, the figures of man, God, and Satan are symbolized, then this can be explained by the fact that both poets have only given a suggestion to their actors and leave it to them to interpret and complete the work according to their own lights.

There are also composers who provide only a suggestion to the performer, who must finish the work. Yes, even the audience is called upon, not merely to understand what the creator has done, but to give ultimate meaning to the work, which without the audience's collaboration would be merely a fragmentary endeavor. Such a procedure has some very questionable aspects; it presupposes an audience of experts, of dramatists or composers, and this, of course, is the ideal of the avant-garde. It is also out of the question that any masterpiece can be created in this manner. The teamwork will display a slightly improvised character, and indeed, improvisation has become central in modern times. But as long as masterpieces are out of reach anyway—because of the missing faith in value—the experiments are interesting and may be the first steps toward a full recovery of creative genius. I think it is a misstatement to explain improvisations as a combination of law and chance. Chance does not belong in a creative work; it was a very questionable element in the absurd (see Chapter IV). What is meant is that in the improvisation, each member is exposed to the inspiration of the other members and to their contributions. This is not chance. The so-called "aleatoric music" would be a monstrosity.

It is a dangerous adventure to interpret the trends of one's own time. Nevertheless, it is necessary to mention and to give a proper place to an endeavor which points to the future and illustrates in its assets, as well as in its shortcomings, the struggle in which human life is involved today. We may thereby throw light upon essential facets of our problem, which we are now taking up again after this short interlude into the questions of the day.

# CHAPTER XI

# Intercession and the Tragic Element

STEP BY STEP, we have tried to reach full understanding of the tragic sacramental life. We even faced the religious concept of incarnation and recognized that its meaning is not mere embodiment but an embodiment with perspective to a sacrificial offering, just as mortality did not mean mere passive exposure to death but a readiness for sacrificial action. Like all fundamental facets of life, incarnation is rooted in the religious realm. The incarnation of Christ as the most powerful example of incarnation was to be regarded not as a mere incorporation to which the Cross was accidentally added but as an incorporation the meaning of which was the Crucifixion and the Resurrection.

Such an incarnation, as a channeling into a task, a role possessing a sacramental nature, is to be seen even in the personality of God. God as a person is a God of action, a God who lives in a task, a Creator-God. The God of the Old Testament, no less than Christ, is a power of doing, and He enters space and time, He enters history, in order to take His place in the communion with man, in the Covenant, which makes Him a partner of His people, guiding them and suffering for them. This is clearly expressed in the Bible, especially by the prophet Hosea. Jehovah is not incarnated in the sense of a corporal embodiment, to be sure, but His life is channeled into a task and He descends into space and time in order to act, to help and to guide as a partner of man on man's level.

A personal God is a sacramental God. Since time immemorial, self-sacrifice has been connected with the Divine Person, in whatever manner this may occur. It is because of this that man is regarded as having been created in the Divine Image. And here we must add another essential attribute of God and of man as persons in a channeled life of action and communion: intercession.

What does "intercession" mean? What does it mean for religious believers? We have been recently told again and again about the importance and uniqueness of the I-Thou relation between men, expounded by the philosophers Fichte and Hegel and adapted to the relation between God and men by Martin Buber. But there is more to it than a mere relation. Intercession enters into it in order to give it the weight and the dignity of its sacramental and even tragic character. The I gives itself to the Thou in a free and responsible decision of sacrifice *intercessionally*. Here the question arises: Before whom is the intercessor responsible? There must be a power or standard with regard to which the responsibility is felt. If we concentrate on the Divine Sacrifice, the sacrifice and intercession of Christ for the sake of mankind, it is obvious that the intercessor and the power before which he intercedes are one and the same person. But this is not yet all. Not only are the intercessor and the power above one and the same person, but the Thou, for whom intercession was made, may become one with the Divine Power. Christ's words, "What you do to the least of My brethren, you do to Me," are a witness to this mysterious unification.

When man rises to the higher level, a reversal of roles is bound to occur, for not only does the human person rise at times to the level of the Divine Power, but the Divine Power may in turn descend and become a Thou, a partner in the communion. In my essay *Logic and Existence* (pp. 145, 148),

I mentioned that God is the principle of love, raised above the communion, unchanging, stable, the center of absolute value, but that He is at the same time a partner *in* the communion, ever newly born and changing in the process of partnership. In His role as partner, the Divine Power is challenged, tried, and sacrificed, and all this for the sake of the sanctification and purification of man, who has become the center of value, the ultimate end of creation.

Theology has been reluctant to acknowledge the intercessional character of God. Relying upon the pagan idea of divine unchangeability and independence, it has greatly missed the beauty and depth of the living God. Freedom was understood as negative only, as "freedom from," as independence, for a dependent God seemed no true object of worship. What was overlooked, however, was the sublime attitude of God's *free* yielding, His *free* surrender to a dependence which, since it was freely adopted, could be freely canceled and was therefore not a real limitation of the Divine Person. Both the God of the Old Testament and Christ yield freely to dependence with regard to Their beloved creatures. There is no love without free yielding, and although such a free dependence implies suffering and sacrifice, this sublime attitude was made the cornerstone of the divine life and its love. It is as the image of such a God that man finds his greatest freedom, again, in a free surrender to those whom he loves. His loyalty, his faith in other people and in a living cause, expressed in his calling, in his vocation, is such a free surrender. Freedom does not act in a vacuum; a free decision is motivated in a specific way, inspired by the value of the beloved object. The unmotivated love which as *agape* was hailed by theologians like Nygren is not love at all but a caricature, a return to the pagan, lifeless, negative freedom of an unchangeable being, unaffected and impassive, like the eternal and abstract system of impersonal truth, all-comprehensive and complete and as such *perfect*, the divinity of pantheism. There is nothing wrong with such a faith; it is the faith of the scientist, but it is definitely not the faith of biblical man, not faith in a trustworthy, loving, and responding God.

Mythology too has avoided the involvement of the higher sphere in man's ever changing and turbulent life, and it has done so at the price of shutting the divine off, petrifying it into an impersonal fate that is separated from the now meaningless and chaotic sphere of human events. But the living and loving God of the Bible is at the root of man's life and is so deeply affected by it that He shares man's existence through suffering, failure, and sacrifice and even allows man to become the meaning of the divine challenge and trial. This is the Christian message, and it has introduced an element of danger in the life of man, who has risen too high and is exposed to the temptation of *hubris*. His rising and the Divine Sacrifice should, however, make man humble, as the sublime figure of Christ did and as the suffering God of Hosea, the repenting God of Jonah, and the challenged God of Job have certainly done. The mystery of the Job story has never been fully clarified, but it is indeed a paradox in this story that God's grandeur rises with the challenge to which He is exposed by Job and that the words which Job uses to glorify this grandeur are the same words which God Himself uses at the end when, in agreement with His challenger, He rejects the submission of the false friends and therefore accepts the challenge as a tribute to His greatness.

Until now, we have discussed the problem of intercession in the religious realm only and have not yet touched upon that intercession which goes on between man and man in the realm of ethics. It is here not God as such but the wider life of communion which is the standard and power before which I and Thou are linked in intercession. We called this wider life of communion the "destiny of man." Although we regarded man as under destiny, ruled by destiny, it may happen that man rises to the level of his destiny, that the interceding I feels responsible to the communion as represented by *itself*. But at times the sublime power before which he is responsible may come to him from his *Thou*, that is, from the very life for which he intercedes. And this is not all. Just as the Divine Power descended onto the level of His creatures, so too in the ethical realm may destiny slip down into the life of its members, challenged, transformed, and reborn in the process of their unfolding. And just as God was both the ruling principle and the partner, so too may communion as destiny be both the ruling power and a challenged and ever newly created structure that is enriched and transformed by the actions of its members.

In the religious realm, we are accustomed to distinguishing between two kinds of intercession by human persons, that of the prophet and that of the saint. The prophet is obviously the intercessor who, together with his people, is subjected to the Divine Power, which is far above him and his people. He is, therefore, *one* with his people, lost like his people, and he must with passionate zeal raise both himself and his people, mold himself and them, in a fierce battle with resisting human material; he must force them and himself into a new mold. Very different is the intercession of the saint. Here the intercessor has risen to the divine level, is himself the intercessor as well as the standard and power of the intercession, so that by his very life and action the grace of fulfillment is granted to his people. No violent molding of the people is here necessary, but the mere holding of a mirror before the people, the mirror of his, the saint's, own life; and if any violence is offered, it is the violence to which the saint lends himself through challenge, trial, and sacrifice in order that grace and justification may come to his people. Christ is the most sublime example of this. And St. Paul sometimes turned from the prophetic intercession to the saintly one, and could cry out: "Not I live, but Christ lives in me." When men speak of "self-realization," it is either an arrogant and immoral attitude, a falling back upon pagan self-enjoyment and self-sufficiency, or it is the saintly sublimation of the intercessor, who knows that what is realized is not his little ego but destiny, the wide self of a holy communion. Without the humility of intercession and responsibility, self-realization is of no avail.

Intercession works in every human dialogue. It is a speaker's listening to a power before which he intercedes for another person and which may reside in the Thou to whom he is speaking or even in the speaker himself. Communication is based on an intercessional communion and experiences the impact of that communion as destiny. The speaker is inspired by his listener, and the listener understands that what is said to him originates in the communion of which he and the speaker are constitutive members. Thus when the I or the Thou rises to the level of the dialogue, embracing both the speaker and the listener, it may happen that the communion as such undergoes a development, is drawn into the dynamic process, is challenged and transformed, maturing in the event. In such a case it assumes a double role: it preserves its ruling and stabilizing power, but it also widens and grows in richness as an unfolding destiny.

It is obvious that in our era of anxiety and absurdity, where the individual is isolated in himself and surrounded in his finitude without a destiny, communication has been regarded as an impossibility. Thinkers have denied man the capacity to enter fully into the lives of others. They have adopted a pagan attitude, a Stoic self-reliance and self-sufficiency, with no bond reaching out to fellow men. Being as such has become the divine, all-comprehensive, and static idea, and man has become the image of this divine isolation. There is no channeling into a dynamic process of action, no task which through intercession and sacrifice leads, under destiny, to the width of a communion of giving and taking. Pantheism is indeed the very antithesis of a sacramental and inter-cessional life, and it excludes both the depth and the height of tragedy. A mere relation between I and Thou, without the power of intercession under destiny, touches only the surface of human communion, a fragmentary interest, a utilitarian bond. The total giving and taking between men presupposes a power before which this act of sacramental living is done and before which responsibility is acknowledged. Wherever it occurs, relation is of a problematic nature. Even the logical relation is a unity which falls apart, a plurality which claims to be one. In the realm of life it is intercession which provides the solution to the problem, intercession before an over-arching structure, a destiny in which men lose themselves in order to regain themselves on a higher and richer level. The pantheistic attitude of self-sufficiency and self-contentment was torn apart by the rebellion of Greek tragedy, where man sacrifices himself in intercession under destiny and draws the lives around him into his tragic orbit. It will now be our task to enter into this extraordinary phenomenon of culture, the great tragedy.

# CHAPTER XII

# The Great Tragic Drama

POETRY IS A presentation of life in its most intensive and most profound form. It does not merely give a symbolic reduction of life or a virtual portrayal, as is believed by some thinkers who see in art nothing but a substitute for real life which somehow points at life and must be interpreted in order to reveal its significance. Poetry and art are neither symbolic nor significant and need no interpretation; with necessity and immediacy, they force the listener or spectator into the depths of life itself, make him live more intensively than he has ever lived in the course of his humdrum existence. Intercession and incarnation, together with sacrifice and responsibility, are the media through which great poetry works and opens the mind and heart of the listener to the depths of human personality and communion.

This is not true of myth, for myth is a device which protects man from responsibility and the free shaping of destiny, significant because it is such a device and interpretative with regard to empirical existence, which in being projected into the mythological pattern receives some meaning and stability. The mythological setting sheds light on the dark and confused sphere of man's struggle and acquits him of decisions of responsible action. Without this fateful setting, life down here on earth is meaningless and like a dream. The mythological setting seems to give life a truth which it does not really have, so that one could call myth a "lie," a label which Nietzsche, confusing poetry with myth, uses with regard to art—a fertile and efficient lie.

But art and poetry are not lies; they concentrate and intensify the truth in life and give it to us in the strongest possible dose. There are different levels of this intensive truth as it unfolds from the primitive myth over epic to drama. In the epic it is still fate which, as a supernatural necessity, protects man from responsibility and free decision, but here man is becoming tired of his childlike innocence and tries to cope with the powers of fate, which, as demons or demonic gods, have intercourse with man, make deals with him, can be bribed, and thus allow man to cooperate in the shaping of his destiny. In the Homeric epic, man starts to free himself, and it was this beginning humanism which endeared the Homeric poem to the Greek nation. There is still enough protection in the rule of fate, raised above man and above the gods, but man can also enjoy some freedom of action, can, with the help of the gods, live his own life. So he has his cake and at the same time is allowed to eat it. It is a transitional state, playful and mixed with doubt and uneasiness, but in spite of this, man can laugh at fate and the gods, although only half-heartedly because he has not yet fully conquered his place in the world.

With the Homeric epic, mythical religion, in its form as divine fate and the life of the gods, has received a deadly blow. The mythological setting begins to crumble, and man seems to emerge out of these ruins a free man, using his wits and his reason in order to shape his life. It looks as if myth had given way to humanism and a pragmatic philosophy, as indeed the Sophists developed it later on. But the Greek genius was not satisfied with such a simple solution; two different trends developed, both substitutes for religion, both serious and profound. One was the Platonic philosophy, which emphasized reason as being divine, a fatelike eternal structure of ideas, worshiped as ultimate reality but negligent with regard to human life; the other trend, in rigid contrast to this solution, was passionately devoted to man, not pragmatic man, but man under destiny—Greek tragedy. It was in tragedy that Greek genius reached its most profound understanding of man, unforgettable and exerting a powerful influence on all subsequent civilizations. More serious than the myth had been, more passionate than any philosophy, Greek tragedy grew out of the myth but transformed it under the auspices of a barbaric god, Dionysus, in the cult of whom the drama unfolded its profound vision of man, of responsible man, of sacrifice and suffering. It appeared in the sky of Greek culture like a bright comet, suddenly and unexpectedly, and disappeared, after a very short time, as suddenly as it had come.

Greek tragedy is of utter seriousness; there is nothing playful about it, nothing arbitrary; there is nothing of escape, no attempt to hide under the broad roof of a fateful setting. There is indeed still a subjection to fate and a more sincere worship of its rule than mythology had bargained for. But fate, far from enslaving man, brings his abilities, urges, and passions to light, makes him more a man than he would have been without the fateful forces which drove him on, so that the hero accepts fate as his destiny, by his free decision adopts the rule of destruction, and claims responsibility for his deeds, although they were laid upon him by necessity.

In the preceding chapters we have tried to characterize what is meant by "man under destiny," mature man, leading a sacramental life, ready to give himself and reaching, by means of his sacrifice, into a wider life of communion. Here man's responsibility includes, intercessionally, all the lives which are near and dear to him. In his tragic action of self-sacrifice, the hero draws into destruction other lives, for which he is responsible.

Insofar as the hero acts under destiny and makes decisions intercessionally for the wider life of his family and friends, he has a role and his life is channeled in order to reach out dynamically into other lives. We have discussed the role and its significance. There is a certain ambiguousness about the role: it can be understood as a reduction instead of a concentration of force, an impoverishment of the infinite possibilities of life instead of an integration of these possibilities into one realization, richer and farther reaching than any and all unrealized possibilities as such. Greek drama has partly surrendered to the ambivalence of the role and has, in its stage technique, petrified and simplified the role to a mask, to a reduction, screening life and exchangeable according to the needs of the moment. This is the price paid for a new and revolutionary discovery, that it sticks to outworn gadgets which are unfit for the new discovery. What had been discovered was the creative and dynamic personality, unknown before, but this person was pictured as a mask, a fictive screen, and the role was conceived as played only, as adopted for the time being and laid aside when not in use. We still speak of the drama as a "play," although there is nothing less playful and more serious than plays are. What had happened was that the unique and profound human personality had been discovered as a concentrated and channeled dynamic force, entering, in its channeled direction, into other lives, other persons, and other roles, and the interplay of these factors revealed a mutual responsibility and intercessional sacrifice, with both responsibility and intercession pointing to a destiny raised above the level of man.

Deep involvement in other lives is our role under destiny, and it was precisely this which Greek tragedy discovered and put into an unforgettable form. Man is not alone; he acts in intercession for others, whom he draws into the fateful course of his action. He hurts and destroys what he loves, but receives dignity and justification for himself and the others in spite of failure and suffering. And we, the spectators, become a part of the communion. We too are drawn into destruction and sublimation; we too are hurt and elated and receive a powerful intensification of life; we too are under destiny; and we too have a role as a channeling of our efforts, thereby reaching beyond our narrow environment. The man who, in old age, has lost contact with other lives has become useless, his existence meaningless. He can be compared to a performer who has acted out his roles and leaves the empty stage. As long as we are alive, we have a role; we are under destiny.

Greek tragedy is the sublime discovery of man's sacrificial and intercessional nature, his involvement in other lives, which he must hurt but which, through sacrifice and suffering, he leads to a more meaningful future. And we, the spectators, are drawn into this communion by awe and compassion. But, as is to be expected, the sudden first appearance of the great tragedy in Greece retains some features of its childhood. There is still much of mythological fate present, a necessity, aloof from human responsibility. The gods, as the messengers and managers of mythological fate, assume a hostile, demonic, ambivalent, and unreliable character: they trick and cheat man into misfortune, entangle him in the net of their lies and half-truths. In Aeschylus' *Prometheus Bound*, even Zeus is portrayed as a cruel demon who has ungratefully taken advantage of his former adviser and has in the vilest way abused Ino, his mistress. With Sophocles, this attitude toward Zeus changes, but not so with regard to other gods; the glorious daughter of Zeus, Athena, displays a malicious joy when the unhappy hero, Ajax, is darkened by insanity.

The demonic nature of the supernatural powers is dwindling, however. Aeschylus at times ascends to a more trusting attitude. In *Oresteia*, Zeus is the guarantor of truth, although a certain doubt still prevails as to Zeus' nature and reliability: "If to the Unknown that name of many names seems good." Furthermore, it is Apollo who leads Orestes to disaster but also helps him out of it. The Erinyes, cruel demons of revenge, are transformed into the Eumenides, well-disposed goddesses, and everywhere the iridescent nature of the gods is shown serving the ambivalent power of fate.

Hand in hand with the complexity of fate and the divine character goes insight into the equally conflicting trends of human personality. Man is not as naïve and simple as mythology and epic wanted him to be. There is something demonic in man, but he also possesses kindness and love. Clytemnestra is a murderess, but she displays both sadistic cruelty and mother love; it is mother love which, hurt by her husband's political use of their daughter, Iphigenia, as a victim to placate the gods and secure success in his state affairs, drives the queen to the murder of Agamemnon. Likewise, it is his devotion to his murdered father which compels Orestes to avenge his father by killing his mother. With Sophocles, the nobility and purity of the hero becomes still more conspicuous. Oedipus is neither a brutal murderer nor a revenger, but is drawn into his deeds by circumstances which he does not fully grasp. He shows himself as a great king and loving husband and father, but he becomes entangled in a net of accidental happenings—accidental with regard to his will and knowledge but necessitated by fate. And when at last he understands, he assumes full responsibility for what has happened and executes the terrible punishment of blinding himself. Antigone too is a noble person bent on fulfilling the duties which religion prescribes and exposing herself courageously to the penalty of death. In both cases, the destiny of the hero draws other lives with him into destruction, and again he is innocent, although responsible. Destiny as the wider setting of life unites with the hero all those near and dear to him and makes them suffer with him under the same destiny. There is, however, a certain rigidity in Oedipus' behavior, as well as in Antigone's fanaticism, but this is by no means a flaw of character and is surely not instrumental for sacrificial suffering. The hero is human, and as a human being has deficiencies of character. But these are not the cause of his downfall. It is rather his nobility and unconscious desire for sacrifice which lead him to death and destruction. His courage, his conviction, and his passionate devotion are instrumental to his tragic destiny. Cowardice would perhaps allow him to escape, but he is dimly aware of a duty which links him to other lives and motivates him to decide freely and to assume responsibility. To be sure, fate has already decided, but in the framework of the fateful setting which the hero adopts as *his* destiny, as *his* own decision, he continues to fulfill in free action what destiny has decreed. Antigone buries her brother and takes her life; Oedipus, with his intrepid searching brings the hidden disaster to light and then blinds himself as his own free executor. Orestes refuses to hide behind the doings of Apollo, and Apollo himself declares that Orestes bears part of the responsibility. Even Clytemnestra is not a passive victim of the curse laid upon the Atreus family. She takes fate into her own hands, risks and sacrifices freely, and thus Orestes can cry out to her: "This Thyself will slay thyself, not I."

In spite of the sublime discovery of man's noble freedom and responsibility, Greek tragedy still adheres to mythological chance, supplementing in the human sphere that which is necessity in the sphere above. Accidents as such are untragic; they are sad and meaningless. Thus the accidental meeting of Oedipus with his father and the latter's subsequent death would be nothing but a distasteful accident—and Oedipus would be right to deny responsibility for such an accidental happening—if the working of destiny would not bring the hero and his father into a living communion so close and so powerful that it is not important how much the doer knew; it is enough that his action destroys a life united to him by destiny and draws his own life into a fateful destruction. We may call the act of the tragic hero a self-sacrifice, and we may ask how much intellectual discrimination enters that act. Is the doer clearly aware of his motivation? No. His death may spring from his way of life, but not in a rational or even causal manner; it results from free decisions made under destiny, that is, decisions which originate in a wider setting, perhaps a blood-communion, and draw all of the lives in that communion into the destruction of the hero. Is this necessity? Is it freedom? The hero does not reflect and ponder; for him and the spectators touched by the drama, there is an inevitable bond between the hero's decisions and the fate of the lives in his orbit.

Even so, Greek tragedy plays up the accidental element in a conspicuous way in order to make the spectator aware of some mysterious power beyond rational motivation and of the irrational working of fate. But what seems to be accidental is not really accidental, and the hero will not regard it as such. He will assume full responsibility, even for accidents, because what comes into focus in these irrational occurrences is ultimately rooted in his destiny; it is as if his being forced things to happen, and he cannot shirk responsibility and punishment for what happened. He did not know and did not will the events, but his ego, with its knowledge and will, is not important; what is important is the objective setting, and once enlightened about this setting, about the hidden threads woven between him and others, he must suffer the consequences of agony and self-sacrifice. Tragic suffering is rooted in knowing, and whether, as Aeschylus puts it, suffering leads to knowledge, πάθος μάθος (suffering-knowledge)— "through tears and dole comes wisdom over the unwilling"— or whether, as Sophocles believes, knowledge is first and suffering follows, it is the unbreakable unity of suffering and knowledge which is the meaning of man's tragic existence. Sacrificial destiny, revealed by sorrowful wisdom, is expressed by Odysseus in Sophocles' *Ajax* when he says, "Naught else are we but mere phantoms, all we that live, mere fleeting shadows," repeating almost verbatim what King David cries out to his people in his abdication speech: "We are strangers before Thee, O God, and sojourners as were our fathers; our days are as a shadow and there is no abiding" (I Chronicles 29:15). But—and this must be added to both of these statements—in spite of the strangeness of our shadowy existence, we are the bearers of our destiny, called upon to assume responsibility.

Death is not the only sacrificial act in Greek tragedy. For Agamemnon, Clytemnestra, and Antigone it is, but not for Orestes and Oedipus. The manner in which these two tragic figures face their destiny is different and shows a certain development in the art of tragedy. Orestes' self-sacrifice is fulfilled in the terrifying experience of suffering before and after the murder of his mother. Suffering purifies him and changes him from a victim of fate to its executor. But Aeschylus is not satisfied with this spiritual transformation; it must be confirmed by a court procedure in which justice is done. Although it is carried out with the assistance of a goddess, the procedure introduces a wrong note into the tragedy and is felt as an anticlimax. Very much more adequate is

Sophocles' solution in *Oedipus at Colonus*. There is no court and no acquittal. In a mysterious way, grace comes to the aged hero, who, purified by long suffering, is lifted from his earthly existence to a beyond which no words can describe and which is the Greek version of a resurrection after the cross has been patiently born; and the spectators share in the purification and elation.

Aristotle regards compassion and terror as the fundamental emotions of tragic purification. Here, however, we should not confuse terror with anxiety, which is overemphasized in modern thinking. Anxiety is untragic; it may be found in those characters who live and act on the periphery of the drama, but not in the central hero. Jocasta is shaken by anxiety and takes her life because she cannot bear her destiny; so also is Ismene, the sister of Antigone, full of anxiety and thus refuses to share in the risk of burying her brother. But most conspicuous is anxiety in the chorus, which accompanies the tragic development with commentaries. Here a group of average people, involved in happenings too great for them to understand and to bear, is indeed shaken by fear. In the economy of Greek drama, the chorus must perform several tasks. It manifests the foil of human weakness, not hardened in the fire of suffering but a raw material, although not without intelligence and at times expressive of problematic man. The chorus is also a residue of mythical craving for security, submitting to fate and resigned in irresponsibility and unfreedom: " Who craves a long life is a fool. Not to be born is best, next best is to leave with speed " (Chorus, *Oedipus at Colonus*). Both reasons for the existence of a chorus disappeared when man fully identified himself with his destiny, leaving no room for problematic anxiety or resigned subjection to a distant fate.

What the hero in Greek tragedy realizes only at the height

of crisis and what his environment scarcely ever realizes, the widening of life so that it embraces fate as its destiny, became the mainspring of modern tragedy. Here, under the impact of biblical prophetic vision, a new kind of man entered the scene, a man openly called to shape his destiny freely in responsibility and self-sacrifice. It is the Shakespearean tragedy which is the most sublime form of the free sacramental and intercessional life of modern man.

Fate, providence, a superrational necessity, is by no means absent in Shakespearean tragedy. Even the stars are introduced, pointing to a mystery that is not resolvable by rational understanding and mere psychological motivation. But nowhere is fate conceived as a predetermining curse or rule which reduces man to a mere object and victim of its determination. That Greek tragedy moved away from such a mythological setting for man and rebelled in the name of freedom and responsibility has been mentioned above, but it remained in an ambiguous twilight between freedom and chance and necessity. The Shakespearean tragedy goes full course and acknowledges that man is responsible for his destiny, which calls him into freedom and comes to him, not from a distant mythological sphere, lifeless, impersonal, and indifferent to man's suffering, but from the living communion of lives, in which it mysteriously works, widening man's self-centered motivation by merging him into an interplay of forces, never totally predictable, although never exposing man to mere chance. In this way the power of myth is broken once and for all. Tragedy has become the untainted presentation of life, but of life under destiny, that is, life meaningful and dignified because it knows itself as called to sacrifice by the wider life of which it is a member. The immense power which Shakespearean tragedy exerts upon us results from the fact that here no translation from an obsolete text, from a mythical tradition, is necessary; instead, we see our own lives revealed to us as we are called to our decision of sacrifice by that very power out of which we live and receive our meaning.

All tragedy is rooted in religious soil. This was undoubtedly true of Greek tragedy, which sprang from the cult of the god Dionysus. The Shakespearean tragedy is equally, if not to a higher degree, religious. This has often been denied, and it is true that God is not mentioned much on the stage. Nevertheless, the mystery and complexity of the human situation, man's embeddedness in a wider life, is nowhere put forth with such power as in Shakespeare's tragedies. Nobody who is exposed to Hamlet, Lear, or Macbeth can avoid the feeling that he is faced with life beyond the everyday level, that man is shown struggling in a darkness which originates not in man himself but in a wider and more powerful sphere, and that man is lifted, through sacrifice and suffering, above this darkness, not merely by his own doing but by a grace which comes from a mysterious realm, a realm of destiny. From act to act the hero is led deeper into the agony of a sacrificial offering, into a destruction which is ultimately self-destruction, and the wisdom behind all of these happenings is that man is not an isolated entity but lives a close communion, so close that in hurting others he finally hurts and destroys himself. What else occurs in the drama *Hamlet* but the unfolding of suffering and self-sacrifice through five acts, accompanied by a steady maturing of personality and wisdom until the hero is ripe for the offering which lifts him and the spectator to a higher sphere? King Lear, rash and overbearing as a despot, is slowly lowered, step by step, until, in utter nakedness and humility, he is exposed to the ultimate trial and sacrifice, the death of his beloved daughter, a death into which he himself is drawn and by which he rises, purifying and lifting us into an intensified life of courage and faith.

Even Macbeth, entangled in the meshes of his dark destiny, gropes his way through blood and tears, hand in hand with a wife he loves and who in her love tumbles into the same darkness, until first she and then he find their fulfillment in the sacrificial destruction to which the deaths of Duncan and Banquo have paved the way.

What is meant here by the self, which is the object of sacrifice? Can we exclude Duncan, whose virtues Macbeth deeply feels and praises? Can we exclude Banquo, his friend and comrade? No. The widened self, which is purified by sacrifice and restored to a new reality, includes all of these lives, intricately united, and the widened communion of lives in their fateful intercourse is the destiny under which the hero acts and dies. The hero is responsible and intercedes for all persons who are affected by his doings; he is their representative, and he represents them responsibly before that holy widened self of the communion. When we proceed to other tragedies, as, for instance, *Othello*, we find the same union of lives: Othello in close contact with Desdemona, united in death, the first death drawing the second into its wake with inner necessity. Even the villain, Iago, is included in this widened setting of destiny and self-destruction; even he serves the fulfillment of the tragic offering, just as Judas, as an indispensable force, belongs to Christ's fulfillment of a sacrificial destiny. We can, of course, neatly separate the good from the bad, the angels from the devils, and we can, with pedantic satisfaction, recognize that crime receives its punishment. But such an attitude of the courtroom is inadequate. We are not allowed to sit in judgment where we ourselves are involved, and this is exactly what tragedy reveals: we are all part of that wide self of communion; we are drawn into the destiny of the hero and share his responsibility. It is the genius of Shakespeare's art which affects our own lives, shaking us out of our indolence and making us aware of the bond between all men.

But tragedy does not merely draw us into the dark abyss of destruction together with the hero and his victims; it also lifts us, purified and strengthened, out of the abyss and opens to us a new and better life. Therefore, the tragic hero is more than a criminal. Aristotle saw, correctly, that nobility must characterize the hero and that nobility must shine through the hero's terrible deed. And the same is true of Shakespeare. The monster Macbeth and even the worst of all, Richard III, carry a halo, and this halo is not justly described by a psychological quality, such as courage or energy; it is the deeply rooted awareness of self-sacrifice, of a living unity between them and their victims. In other words, it is their destiny which sends them into the "yellow leaf," a necessity not like a mythical curse, but of an instinctively experienced unity which is a force in them and above them, a force of symbiosis, of an interplay of inseparable living careers, a unity which, however, they freely accept, for this widened realm of destiny gives them dignity and finally grace. There is martyrdom in the tragic hero, and there is a certain failing, not in the sense of legal guilt, but caused by a cosmic deficiency manifested in man and in conflict with a responsibility which is too wide for man to carry out and which involves man—in its all too comprehensive scope—in disaster and suffering. Shakespeare and Dostoyevsky both reject justice, and although one of Dostoyevsky's works carries the title *Crime and Punishment*, it is precisely in this novel that courtroom procedure and human judgment lose their meaning. Imprisonment hardens and revolts the hero, while it is the understanding and love of his bride, an understanding of his destiny, which opens the hero for the grace pouring into his heart as the ultimate fulfillment of his tragic existence.

Some thinkers have denied that there is a tragic element in Christian faith because, in their opinion, salvation excludes tragedy from a life fulfilled in grace. But the opposite is true and must be stated firmly. Tragedy fulfills itself in salvation. It is the healing of the mythological schism between an impersonal fate and man's life, the close interaction of a living God and living men, which has brought destiny down into the sphere of man's action, so that man can now rise to the level of his destiny and be reborn by his suffering. On the other hand—and this is exactly what the Christian faith has done to tragedy—in modern drama, destiny itself receives a new and ever new meaning through man's suffering and sacrifice. In modern tragedy, in the tragedy of Shakespeare and his followers, destiny is not simply an unchanging power; it grows in the procedure of the drama, a dynamic, ever enriched setting, not to be pinned down in a definition, but experienced throughout the process of dramatic action, unfolding together with the hero's development and fulfillment. Therefore, the fundamental Greek motto of tragedy, that through suffering comes knowledge, knowledge of the fate beyond, is now changed. Knowledge is not enough; discovery may be a part of the total experience, which, however, is a doing rather than a knowing, action rather than discovery, a *shaping* of *destiny*, a *creative adventure*. It is this transformation of destiny which brings grace to the hero, a grace which, through the gloom of agony, radiates and lifts both the hero and the spectator into the blessing of this widened, enriched, and purified destiny.

Shakespeare has wisely introduced many mysterious elements into his tragedies in order to lead the spectator away from a narrow psychological interpretation and point to a wider realm. He has taken refuge in the elementary powers of nature, in storms, lightning, and thunder, in the derangement of the human mind in madness; he has even brought witches and ghosts onto the stage, although his era had outgrown belief in such forces. He has done all of this in order to create an atmosphere of superhuman, superrational necessity, to which the inevitable flow of time is added: "Look into the seeds of time and say which grain will grow and which will not," or, "All yesterdays have lighted fools the way to dusty death."

It is the mystery of destiny which Shakespeare wishes to awaken in the minds of the hero and the spectator. We shall not make the mistake of explaining scientifically the deeds of the hero, either by conscious motivations of a psychological kind or by unconscious drives of the Freudian id, by Oedipus complexes and similar devices of our intelligence, an intelligence which in Shakespeare's time, the Renaissance era of scientific rationalism, began to replace and outgrow belief in superrational powers. It is not probable that Shakespeare wanted his audience to believe in the reality of witches and ghosts; instead, he left these demonic creatures in the twilight of doubt, and he did not make them instrumental for the course of events, as Greek drama did. The ghost of Darius in *The Persians* and the ghost of Agamemnon, approached by Orestes and Electra, in *Choephoroi* bring the dramatic action into flux, but in *Hamlet* the ghost of Hamlet's father is introduced in order to show the complexity of the hero's action, motivated not merely by sensible, rational considerations or by emotions, clearly to be labeled, but driven by ineffable powers which work in the turbulent interaction of human lives, never quite predictable and forcing the hero into his destiny. The procrastination which seems to be prominent in Hamlet's attitude is not caused by a weakness of character or by too much reflective thinking; in fact it is not procrastination at all, but the slow and relentless working of Hamlet's destiny, bringing him, step by step, nearer to his fulfillment, which is ultimately his self-destruction, drawing into it all those who are near and dear to him, blood relatives and friends alike. But out of this holocaust rises a purified life, a Hamlet, a Gertrude, even a Claudius, who, pitted against each other in tragic antagonism, find their unity of communion beyond death and destruction, and it is the father's ghost who somehow sublimates this communion, expressing the other-worldly aspect of the realm of destiny.

A procrastination similar to that in Hamlet's behavior seems to work in Macbeth. If he were just a murderer instead of a man under destiny, he would have done, without scruple, what ambition compels such a man to do—like Laertes, who is untragic and as such is opposed to the tragic hero, Hamlet. Like Laertes, Macbeth would have used violence and tricks without hesitation in order to realize his purpose. This would have been perfectly good psychology. But good psychology is not enough. The hero stands for more than his narrow self; he unites in himself the lives of many, thinks for many and thus thinks in complex and contradicting ways, feels for many, and, in compassion with his victims and love for those he must destroy, finally dies, when the time has ripened, in the deaths of those he has destroyed. "Ripeness is all," "Readiness is all"—again and again Shakespeare points to the wisdom of a slow and tragic unfolding which at last reaches its peak.

There are accidents here and there in Shakespeare's dramas, but they are of minor importance and do not carry the weight which accidents possessed in Greek tragedy. It is indeed an accident that Edmund forgets the message to have Lear and Cordelia both killed, so that when they are found, only Cordelia is murdered, while Lear is still alive. It is an accident that Desdemona loses her handkerchief. All this,

however, is not of decisive importance and melts into nothing
in the face of destiny and its power. One should not emphasize
the accidental and see it even where it is not meant to be
found. Lear's astonishing blindness in the opening act is as
little an accident as the equally astonishing silence of
Cordelia. Both are fenced in by blindness and silence, and
in this essential loneliness, they tragically point toward each
other and toward their union in death.

Shakespeare has no reason to use accidents or sudden
revelations of truth in the same manner in which Sophocles
did and had to do. Shakespeare's truth reveals itself
slowly and in degrees through the power of sorrowful acts.
Every moment of agony brings the hero to a deeper understanding of his destiny. Suffering and knowing are one and
the same act, and both are caused by the free and responsible
decision of the hero, free in responding to the call of his
destiny. In this way, Macbeth in the atmosphere of storm and
witchcraft, Hamlet in the atmosphere of ghostly appearance,
and Lear in storm and madness realize their destiny in self-
sacrifice. No anxiety shakes the sorrowful knower on his
road to destruction. Neither Hamlet nor Lear nor Macbeth is
at any moment exposed to anxiety. As in Greek drama, only
the nontragic figures are shaken by fear before they disappear
in the great holocaust which the hero's deed has kindled:
Gertrude, Claudius, Ophelia, Banquo, Gloucester. The man
under destiny, however, firmly but slowly follows his course
of action with an inevitableness which is rooted in his *amor
fati*, in his resolve not to shrink back from his destiny. That
he must ultimately destroy himself is known to the hero with
that somnambulistic certainty which by degrees develops
into conscious clarity. Macbeth knows about the "yellow
leaf" into which his life will lead from the first moment of
decision; Hamlet knows it when he decides to follow the call

of his father's ghost; Lear, first blinded by vanity, knows it
when misfortune has torn the kingly garments from his body.

All this is obvious. What is difficult to grasp, however, is the
ultimate outcome and meaning of it. How does the resurrection follow the cross? Shakespeare is shy when it comes to
this point. His tragedies end in some triviality, in a kind of
restoration of common sense or political balance. But this is
his way of covering up the deeper truth in order that the
audience may find its own approach and enter on its own
solution, which may convert disaster into grace. It would
perhaps go too far and be too simple to use the biblical
approach and see a final grace in the all-embracing love shin-
ing through blood and tears. It would be too simple. Any
interpretation would be too simple. But something of this
kind, unspoken, is at the bottom of the great Shakespearean
tragedy. It is more clearly expressed in *King Lear* than in
other tragedies. What triumphs in the love of Lear and
Cordelia, in the love of Edgar and his father, Gloucester, is
the power which has sent them into suffering and death and
which is kindled in the audience. Some minor poets have
tried to change the end of this drama, saving Lear's and
Cordelia's lives and uniting them in a sequence of happy
years together. This will not do. The tragedies in our lives
may be consummated in the purification which suffering
provides and may allow us to live on in order to reap the
fruits of our suffering and sacrifice. But poetic tragedy is of
such an intensity that it throws life into a new dimension
which is not available in mere continuation on the same level.
Everything is over-life-sized, including emotions, aspirations,
and ultimately the sacramental offering. Here that total
giving which is death is needed to put its seal on man's tragic
life, gathering into one irreparable deed all which life held and
had to give.

That love is also the last word in tragedies like *Macbeth* and *Richard III* is not easy to prove. We have, however, pointed out that Macbeth destroys lives with which he is united in love and draws other beloved lives into his self-destruction. As to King Richard III, we may mention that it was neglected love which, burning and wounding him, drove this hero into his destruction (see *Henry VI, Part III*, Act III, scene 2), and it is shortly before his death that he confesses his longing for love, a longing perverted and turned into revenge (*Richard III*, Act V, scene 3).

But however this may be, it is safer to leave untouched the mystery which widens the scope of our life, involves us in sorrow and sacrifice, but ultimately lifts us into the higher sphere prepared by our destiny.

# CHAPTER XIII

# History and Work

THE IMPORTANCE OF sacrifice as the core of man's life cannot be overemphasized. From the moment of our maturity we recognize, as the meaning of our life, the sacramental devotion which illuminates our path. We know that we must perpetually give from ourselves, from the accumulated treasure of the past, and that we must give in response to a demand, a call which may come to us from the future or from a similarly vast and indefinite realm which we may call "world" or, more humbly, the "request of the day."

What we are less clearly aware of is the intercessional aspect of our sacrifice. We are not alone when we act in a sacramental manner; we stand for more than our own little sphere. We represent, but we do not represent abstractly or symbolically, as an instance represents a law or a particular represents a universal; nor are we representatives of the genus man. We are representing something concrete and individual: a communion of lives of which we are members. We make this concrete representation by sacrificing, by giving ourselves without restraint, motivated by the communion and its needs and turned toward it as the beneficiary of our action, interceding *for* the communion as well as *before* the very same communion. This idea is clearly set forth in the great poetic tragedy, where the self-sacrifice of the hero includes the lives with which he is in touch, draws them into his sacramental act, and sublimates, purifies, and intensifies these lives from whence the call came and toward which the call reached.

Here, then, it dawns upon man that the world toward which he had aspired in the awareness of his own deficiency—always remote from the faraway, clouded, and unreachable world—that this very world is perpetually rising before him as the meaning and destiny of his life and that it is the living communion toward which his sacrifice is directed. As a man under destiny he is united with this world, neither, however, thrown into the world nor merely aspiring in anxiety toward it as a distant and unreachable realm. The colloquial expression "to be *in* the world," as if the world were a receptacle, a spatial medium, is misleading. We are *in* the world insofar as the world of a living communion is the power which, in intercessional action, drives the agent from the past as well as a motivating force and which also calls from the future as the meaning and fulfillment of his action and thus seems to surround him from all sides and to give him his mediating place, not in a static space, but in the dynamic process of a sacramental action. Lives which were a part of his past drive the agent into his daring and sacrificing adventure, become involved in the ensuing destruction, and raise him to a higher sphere which again—but now as the meaning and destiny of the action—is the very communion for which he acted and before which he is responsible as a purified and intensified life.

What was revealed in the life of the tragic hero is the life of every responsible person under destiny, in the world, inspired and motivated by the world of living people, sacrificing himself for them and rising with them out of his sacrifice to that higher life whence the call came. Thus the life of man under destiny is a life of service, and the offering of service is a total giving, which may be death but which can also be any unlimited devotional self-giving. No limited project suffices, for all projects are taken back into the service, which cannot be fulfilled, ended, but continues infinitely. Ever new decisions will have to be made for this infinite service, which was motivated by a source wider than the psyche of the agent and which was responsible to a destiny wider than that of the doer. In other words, the man under destiny is historical man.

History has structure and meaning, but this meaning cannot be abstracted and conceptualized. It lives in the bearer of history, inspires him, and motivates his actions, which are actions of self-sacrifice; but as long as it is alive in him, it cannot be defined. Historical meaning is unique and shapes the history of the historical individual, which is at the same time the history of the widened communion, for which and before which, interceding, the bearer of history acts.

It is life in its widened form of communion, not death, toward which man, especially historical man, lives. Heidegger's gloomy statement is false. Were death the destiny of man, then history would indeed be the "terror" of which Eliade speaks, the terror of unfreedom (*The Myth of the Eternal Return*, pp. 140 ff.). In contrast to the terror of history, Eliade develops his own glorification of mythology, as if it were a liberation. The opposite, however, is true. History as the continuous service to a living ideal, in free decision under the call of destiny, is a manifestation of man's responsibility, while myth is the expression of a predetermining law of fate under the impact of which man pursues his life as a victim of necessity. His freedom is exhausted in the mere projection of his life process into *illud tempus*, into that supertemporal eternal stretch of the mythological narrative. We explained this facet of mythology as an attempt to gain security, to escape from responsibility and from the freedom of historical man. There have been periods in the history of man when the unfolding of the unique and responsible historical acts was combined with a mythological fixation in timeless eternity, a paradoxical complexity of disparate attitudes. This happened when history became so hard to bear that weak man needed a vacation from history, and relief was provided by a closing of history, by an eschato-logical dream of the end of history, a vague and empty mythological addition to the process of historical unfolding. What had originally been the Kingdom of God *in* history and *through* the responsible working of men under destiny was turned by frightened people into a kingdom *at the end* of history, replacing history with a hazy dream of mythology and putting off man's responsible action by means of an eschatological paradise. A similar escape characterizes the Buddhist despair over the unbearable suffering in life's unfolding. Here the historical and responsible actions of Karma were terminated in nirvana, which, as an empty dream of mythology, ultimately canceled everything life had provided, including even Buddha and his teaching.

Very different is courageous and responsible reliance on history, ever newly created by free decisions that do not originate in a vacuum but are responses to a call which is renewed in every life and which asks for a renewed response on the part of historical people. Thus in Deuteronomy (5:2–3 and 30:19) man is not asked to look back on a mytho-logical past or forward to the end of history but is called to immediate action: "God is with us who are all of us *here* alive *this* day." And on "*this* day" God has set before man life and death between which to choose.

The historical life is a responsible and a sacramental life, and what is especially important, it is an intercessional life. We have emphasized this point, and we have drawn attention to the fact that as an intercessor the historical agent bridges the past with the future—the past as a trust with the future as destiny and meaningful realization—and it is the people who are both the trust and the destiny, the trust *for* which and the destiny *before* which man feels responsible. The latter statement may be doubted, but we pointed to Christ's testimony when He revealed that the least of His brethren had taken his place as divine destiny, as the tribunal before which responsible man was to act and to serve. Both demands originate in the people as a creative source: the demand to mold, to raise, to lift out of the rot of the past, and the demand to acknowledge as meaning and destiny these same people, now risen to the height for which the sacrificial act prepared them. Thus not a projection into a strange and distant *illud tempus* is demanded, as in mythology, but the historical action perpetually creates its supertemporal meaning in the tension of intercession, devoted to the past and carrying it into the future, both held together and integrated by the same living entity, the holy people, for which and before which responsible historical man carries out his sacramental decision. It is in this way that historical man transcends his temporal action and reaches continuously into the supertemporal meaning of destiny, which stretches as an eternal present over past and future. Historical man is therefore immortal man, that is, a man who by his devotion and sacrifice lives and transcends his death. The finitude which Heidegger emphasizes in historical man—because he fences man in between birth and death—is a reduction of history, not only to the lawful structure of biology, but also to the petrified fate of mythology, where birth and death become important. Historical man is infinite, immortal man, and the praise of his name through the ages illustrates only what is inherent in his very action.

Another serious fallacy is the existentialist emphasis on repetition, which also points to mythology and its rituals. There is no repetition of the past in the present or in the future. What is characteristic for the intercessional historical act is that past and future are welded into one indivisible present, which is unique, ever new, and incomparable. Even the understanding of history is not an act of repetition: by means of his ingenious imagination, the historian enters into the unique and unrepeatable process of a present, elucidates it in its uniqueness, and gives himself entirely to it, disappearing as a separate person in his task. That the historian himself has his own history is of importance only insofar as it enables him to understand the history in which he is interested; only a human being can understand history. But it would be a crucial mistake and a falsification of history if the historian were to mix his own needs and wishes into the grasp of the history he is describing. It is therefore wrong that every historiography gives a different picture, because of the ever present other destiny of the writer. If this were so, no written history would be true and the different versions would clash with that unique ideal which the bearers of history serve and which they usually close into a living ideal person, a god, or a legendary hero, just as the Jews found in Jehovah and His covenant the ultimate meaning of their sacramental service. The historian's imaginative reshaping of history would substitute a new, modern, and false ideal and would have to invent another personification, or at least would have to give to the beloved person or god or hero new trends of character.

But the *bearer* of the historical process himself, as intercessor, will indeed shape history in his own unique way according to his understanding of the historical intercession. He may emphasize the molding of the past and see in the people a trust which drives him passionately toward the future, including the projection of his own deficient person into the deficient past, fanatically encroaching upon the people and forcing them into their higher destiny, as the *prophets* did; or he may, as intercessor, be close to the fulfilled destiny and in a *saintly* way disappear in the fulfilled ever present meaning, leaving the people to their own ways of reaching salvation after he has set, once and for all, the sacramental pace for those who can follow. But whether as prophet or as saint, the intercessor will listen to a call which comes to him from his destiny, and in listening he will speak, so that a perpetual dialogue will continue between him and the people who are his trust and at the same time his destiny. The listening to the call and the calling itself will meet in the agent as one and the same act, under destiny, and it is in Kant's sublime moral philosophy that this paradox finds clear expression as the paradox of a listening to the moral law, identical with the free act of *giving* this very law. Historical man is indeed moral man; there is no difference between the two if history is understood as a sacramental action under destiny.

Therefore, morality too is strengthened by tragedy and self-sacrifice, by intercession and service. What is called "moral law" is not an abstract structure but the concrete and unique communion of love, which, because it is lived, is perpetually renewed and which molds us when we sacrifice, not our inclinations, as Kant taught, but our whole being, which, however, is restored in our sacrifice and lifted into a higher sphere, including and carrying with it the lives within our reach.

History as cultural history is as much religious history as it is ethical, scientific, and artistic history; it is also, but to a lesser degree, political history. Political history is often distorted and diverted from its true service by environmental happenings, so that an organized collective must watch rigidly and typically, subjecting the lives of the people to abstract law in order to keep the process straight. Sociology, with its typical attitude, will therefore be a more adequate elucidation of politics than history. Group life, the average natural man with his typical cravings, will be the topic of sociology, which is more interested in the repeatable facets of life than in the unique service of its unfolding. What Greek history tried to reveal was, as Thucydides frankly admits, the ever unchanging nature of *homo politicus*; his writings were directed to and took as subject matter *homo politicus*, and his purpose was to reveal ever unchanging human nature and the ever repeated mistakes it makes in political action, not any unique and incomparable occurrence of human behavior. This interest in the structure of human nature as such and human society as it remains unchanged throughout the centuries reveals the genus man in mental and lawful stability, not the unique individual life of people under destiny, which is the true concern of history and culture, ever new, incomparable, and creative.

It will be at the height of culture that historical communion reaches a stage where every person acts responsibly under destiny, each taking care of every other person, each interceding as well as becoming an object of intercession, with no one being simply a follower of a prophet, but with each person possessing a prophetic spirit. In the history of religion, ethics, and art, such golden epochs of culture have indeed been recognized and venerated, each member of the communion giving himself to every other in his actions. To be a prophetic people was the ideal of the Jews, and it meant that every member interceded and took the responsibility for all; to love your neighbor and every neighbor was the same ideal, now in the perspective of ethics. The medieval craftsman in his guild was an example of all-embracing responsibility in the field of art, with every worker doing his very best, not for reasons of competition, but for the sake of better service to the group and its culture. Here no typical acts are asked for, as in political history, but highly individual and unique sacramental deeds. Education should follow this idea of a mutual, all-embracing intercession. It should not prepare students for success in competition or for excellence in order to stand out above others; instead, it should imbue students with the spirit of intercession for all, and it should develop qualities that are fit for such service, responsibility, and sacrifice.

History unfolds in time and involves the whole man, body and soul, realizing itself in situations and crystallizing into specific works to be done, that is, finite and planned achievements. However, works may become a serious danger for the continuous process of history; the agent may become arrested in his achievements, become proud of them, and may regard his service as fulfilled. The conflict between faith and works in religious history and between love and works in ethical history has been violent at times and has led to the fanaticism of total rejection of works in these fields. But here we must face the complexity of human nature, which, involved in infinite service, nevertheless must settle down in finite works, risk the danger of getting stuck in them, and, with untiring effort, transform them into steppingstones for the advancement of unending service. Such a transformation of potential arrest into means of intensifying and continuing a dynamic forward drive can only be made in the spirit of sacrifice; here again, sacrifice and a sacramental life become the purifying power and pave the way to salvation. Works, achievements, must be discarded, not amassed and hoarded, and it is in the sacrificial aspect that our works receive a positive and creative value, intensifying the life of the communion. The Far East has tried a simpler and more radical solution: it has withdrawn from works entirely and has gloried in the inner concentration of an ascetic faith. Such a decision, made once and for all, facilitates a simplified devotion that is available to all; supported by tradition, even the weaker members of a group will be able to follow without fail. The West has pursued a more ambitious goal: it has sought to enclose finite, material accomplishments—a whole world of things and works—within spiritual service in order that the world of things and works may be sanctified and may participate in the spiritual meaning of life. But many have failed in this difficult and dangerous task; they have become stuck in finite works and their short-lived enjoyment, possessed by those things which they had thought to possess, drowning their spiritual ambition in material success, pride, and superficial satisfaction. Too fond of their past and its achievements, these people have shrunk back from sacrifice and from the intensification which sacrifice would have provided. Works are a risk, but when they are sacrificed, they give to life an elation which the total extinction of works has never reached.

In the history of culture, therefore, art plays a prominent role, but not because aesthetic value outshines all other values. It is even questionable whether a specifically aesthetic value exists, or whether what we call "beautiful" is not merely another word for "sacramental," for the intensification which sacrifice provides, residing in and revealed by a certain kind of work, the art-work. Any sacrifice under destiny for a wider life around us is a cultural act and is beautiful. But indeed, most acts are tempted to assume and claim an inherent value of their own, to be cherished for their own sake, hoarded and possessed. The paradox, however, is that the more a work assumes self-importance, the more it slips down into usefulness for the doer's comfort or pride or power as a mere means relative to a low, humdrum existence, as an implement, a tool, a utilitarian object. Only those acts and works are truly valuable which point beyond themselves to a loving communion, embedded in that communion and serving as an expression of the mutual service of its members. They cancel themselves out and vanish in the intensified life of the communion—as the art-work obviously does—as models of a sacramental object. Such works bind their creators to the audience or spectators, carrying all into an intensified process of living communion.

Any work performed for the purpose of intensifying life around it is a cultural act and belongs to history. Therefore, a service which produces sacramental works is termed a "vocation," a "calling," a "profession"—words taken from the religious vocabulary. We "profess" our faith by devoting ourselves without restraint to medical work or to teaching or to other similar works of total devotion. These are "callings" "vocations" because the service they involve calls us to our responsible destiny. Whether we work as artists or scientists or ministers or even as plain factory workers, we have a "calling" to serve with all that we can give. The writer of Ecclesiastes was correct when he said that work done for others is a holy service but that work done in greed and for the sake of power is a curse: "Being alone, for whom do I labor?" (4:8 ff.).

As we mentioned in an earlier chapter, man's isolation is most intensively felt when he is cut off from work which made him a member of a living communion. He will soon disintegrate spiritually and physically. He will die. But there is not much difference between such a person and the man who works in a mechanical routine without the awareness of service, just for the sake of making a living. A man of this kind, even if he is still young and possesses physical strength, will soon age and disintegrate. Man is not meant to be alone; the fruitful soil in which he grows and flourishes is the loving and understanding communion of lives. Without this communion as the destiny of man, work is nothing but a treadmill. The myth of the Danaïdes, who in eternity must fill a bottomless barrel with water, which, poured in from above, flows out at the bottom, is an early expression of such deadening work as a curse. And so is the myth of Sisyphus, who is condemned to roll a heavy rock uphill, only to see it slip from his hands and roll down again before he has reached the top, so that he is forced to start all over again. Greek life must have lacked faith in service, in the joyful communion of giving and taking among men. As a slave-culture it was indeed cut off from the rejuvenating experience of work and service, although one would have expected that the service of the free man in and for the state provided a sacramental life of its own kind. Was it the institution which had taken over and killed the living spirit of intercession and sacrifice?

Besides manifesting a deep melancholy in its mythological narratives, the early Greek mind invented and found a childlike consolation in the playful and irresponsible adventures of its half-gods. The deeds of Heracles are of such a childish character: cleaning the Augean stables, stealing the golden apples, bringing the Hound of Hell to the surface of the earth. All of these adventures, risky in a sportsman's manner, are without any serious value. Adventurous man is another type of lost man who substitutes a false value of sensation and vanity for the true bond between him and his brothers. Greek culture had been sidetracked from the outset; it had lost contact with religion and had found a substitute in philosophy, which, sublime as it was, could not fully replace what religion would have meant to the people. Only the great tragedy, for a very short time, came close to the revelation of intercessional sacramental life and destiny.

Our western culture has been nourished by a profound vision of sacrifice, intercession, and destiny and has grown beyond its beginnings in Greek thought, supplementing the lucid and stable structure of Greek order with the emotional depth of biblical vision. Even so, Western culture has had relapses into the safety of mythology, into the security of power and possession, into acquisitiveness and the enjoyment of egotistic isolation. Franklin's terrible phrase "Time is money" is the expression of a confused generation—even much more depressing than the melancholic mythology of Greece—for here is not regret and an awareness of loss but a cheerful and childlike attempt to make a virtue out of a vice. The agonies of our own era, inflation and world wars, have made us wiser and have taught us an unforgettable lesson: Not money, which runs through our fingers, not power, which degenerates, not pleasure, which becomes boredom, but a life under destiny, sacramental and intercessional, every person giving himself to others without restraint—this alone justifies human existence.

# Bibliography

Only those works which are cited by page or section number in the text are included here.

CAMUS, ALBERT. *Le Mythe de Sisyphe*. Paris: Gallimard, 1942.

DILTHEY, WILHELM. *Gesammelte Schriften*. Vol. V. Leipzig and Berlin: Verlag Teubner, 1924.

ELIADE, MIRCEA. *The Myth of the Eternal Return*. Trans. Willard R. Trask. New York: Pantheon Books, 1954.

EMRICH, WILHELM. *Franz Kafka*. Frankfurt am Main: Athenaeum Verlag, 1960.

FOSS, MARTIN. "Problematik des Geistes," *Logos*, XII (1924).

———. "Probleme der Ethik," *Logos*, XIII (1925).

———. *Logic and Existence*. New York: Philosophical Library, 1962.

FREUD, SIGMUND. *Civilization and Its Discontents*. Vol. XXI of *The Standard Edition of the Complete Psychological Works of Sigmund Freud*. Ed. James Strachey. London: Hogarth Press, 1961.

———. *Collected Papers*. Vol. IV. Ed. Ernest Jones. New York: Basic Books, 1959.

HEIDEGGER, MARTIN. *Being and Time*. Trans. John Macquarrie and Edward Robinson. New York: Harper, 1962.

RILKE, RAINER MARIA. *The Book of Hours*. Trans. A. L. Peck. London: Hogarth Press, 1961.

SARTRE, JEAN-PAUL. *La Nausée*. Paris: Gallimard, 1938.

———. *Being and Nothingness*. Trans. Hazel E. Barnes. New York: Philosophical Library, 1956.

# Index

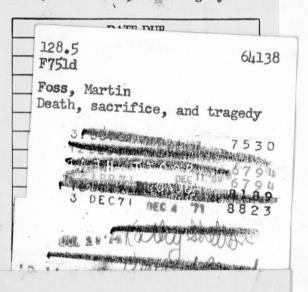